Mothering, God, and the Mothering God

Mothering, God, and the Mothering God

The Relevance of Biblical and Historical Narratives Today

V. Jean Thomas

Foreword by Diane Leclerc

WIPF & STOCK · Eugene, Oregon

MOTHERING, GOD, AND THE MOTHERING GOD
The Relevance of Biblical and Historical Narratives Today

Copyright © 2025 V. Jean Thomas. All rights reserved. Except for brief quotations in critical publications or reviews, no part of this book may be reproduced in any manner without prior written permission from the publisher. Write: Permissions, Wipf and Stock Publishers, 199 W. 8th Ave., Suite 3, Eugene, OR 97401.

Wipf & Stock
An Imprint of Wipf and Stock Publishers
199 W. 8th Ave., Suite 3
Eugene, OR 97401

www.wipfandstock.com

PAPERBACK ISBN: 979-8-3852-4545-1
HARDCOVER ISBN: 979-8-3852-4546-8
EBOOK ISBN: 979-8-3852-4547-5

VERSION NUMBER 09/03/25

Unless otherwise indicated, all Scripture quotations are from New Revised Standard Version Bible, copyright © 1989 National Council of the Churches of Christ in the United States of America. Used by permission. All rights reserved worldwide.

To all the sisters, daughters, friends, and mothers who, like me, are still figuring this all out.

Contents

Foreword by Diane Leclerc | ix
Acknowledgments | xii

1 Mothers Today: How Did We Get Here? | 1
2 Mothers in Christian Scripture | 30
3 Biblical Metaphors of God as Mother | 75
4 Notable Mothers in Christian History | 93
5 Relevant Ramifications for Today's Church | 125

Bibliography | 157

Foreword

MOTHERING IS HARD. THERE might be one mother in a crowd who would disagree. It is hard on a practical level, beginning with giving birth, which we not so ironically call labor. Mothering involves little sleep, nursing/feeding on demand, and hard physical work—the development of "mommy muscles" to literally carry the child for months before it can walk, and then chasing the fearless toddler before it can be taught to stay put. The physical tasks are endless even as the child ages. Place on top of that the pressure of the mother knowing that what kind of person the child develops into is largely up to her. Constant questions. Am I disciplining too much or not enough? What can I do to help my child develop the right values? How do I teach him healthy relationships? How do I teach her about conflict resolution? How do I help them have good self-esteem without creating narcissists? Endless questions. A mother is responsible for raising physically, psychologically, socially, relationally, and ethically healthy children who will grow into healthy adults.

As author Jean Thomas shows, the pressure on mothers today is "intense"! Intensive mothering has become an ideology strongly emphasized in secular society. Media of all sorts stresses that there is a right way to mother and a wrong way to mother (despite that the criteria is changing all the time). All sorts of opinions on what a proper mother does, often competing with each other, set a tone that make the strongest of mothers insecure. Chapter one gives an overview of how we got here. It isn't always pretty.

Beyond the secular standards of mothering, things become even more complex and pressurized in the context of the Christian faith and the environment of the church. On top of that, we find ourselves culturally

Foreword

in a place where we need to ask, Which Christianity? Which church? The polarization of Christianity has perhaps reached an all-time high; Christianity on the right and Christianity on the left are so vastly different that it is perhaps time to talk about American Christianities, instead of one common religion. Conservative Christianity has a particular subculture, often termed "evangelicalism," that has itself changed throughout its history and has even changed in this century. It has very strong opinions about the proper roles of women in general and the role of mother in particular. While secular society has certain expectations for mothers, the expectations on (conservative) Christian mothers is cranked up a hundred fold. It is the responsibility of the mother to raise spiritually strong children and to set a perfect example of what it means to be a wife and mother for the girls in this Christian subculture. The woman is placed in a somewhat paradoxical situation of subordination to men, while at the same time being the person (solely) responsible for the actions and character of her children. In this context, the woman is discouraged from working altogether, while working as a minister is outrightly forbidden. A mother can feel like a subhuman who has immense pressure and responsibility on her shoulders to raise good, even perfect humans. On the more liberal side of the theological spectrum, there is the same pressure on mothers even if the parenting issues stressed can vary.

In this extremely important book, Jean Thomas offers us an accurate, even acute analysis of the situation mothers find themselves in today, especially in the church. She also offers the reader the backstory of how we got here by reviewing mothering in history. Her main premise is that it has not always been like this; there are different paradigms in history available to us. In addition to a review of American history, she offers a chapter of important mothers in history and highlights their emphases and insights. She does the same for women in the Bible as she exegetes the scriptural texts in honest and fresh ways.

The true forte of this book is Thomas's straightforward approach to the topic of God as a mother. Again, she turns to the Bible as a resource and lifts from the pages several key texts that depict God in feminine terms. Besides being biblically accurate, this insightful rendering addresses an issue that has been afoot in the church for the last forty years or so: Is God essentially male? In previous years the question has been taken up by theologians, and specifically by feminist and womanist theologians. But more recently, the issue has moved far beyond speculative theology, and even the concerns of

Foreword

liberation theologians. The question has been taken up by those interested in the field of trauma.

Statistics show that one in three women and one in six men have experienced sexual abuse or assault in their life. The very strong majority of perpetrators are men, and a strong majority of them fit into fathering roles in relation to those they abuse. The statistics do not change for those inside verses outside the church. In addition, the revelations of sexual and spiritual abuse by clergy (again, mostly men) are on the rise.[1] Without a lengthy discussion here, the spiritual imagination that limits the metaphors of God as father and male can limit victims of trauma access to more healing imaginations. Depicting God as mother, which is clearly a biblical option, can be a powerful spiritual resource to those who suffer from the spiritual complexity of relational safety with God. Many need a mothering God.

After these biblical and historical reviews, Thomas returns to the contemporary situation regarding mothering today, indeed the relevant ramifications especially in the context of the church. Her considerations are ultimately practical in the last chapter. She reviews how the church can and should teach, from the Bible, about the true value and roles of mothers. She offers advice on worship, church ministries (including comments regarding her own tradition's affirmation of women's ordination), leadership, and other topics, and gears that advice toward the empowerment of women and mothers—for their sake, and for the health and wholeness of the church itself. It is my privilege to recommend this important book and write its foreword. For Jean Thomas's bravery and ministry through its words and ideas, I am truly thankful.

Rev. Diane K. Leclerc, PhD
Author, theologian, pastor, and mother

---

1. For data related to sexual abuse and assault, see, e.g., UN Women, "1 in 3 Women" and 1in6, "1 in 6 Statistic." See also Leclerc and Peterson, *Side of the Cross*, xv–xvi.

Acknowledgments

Mothering can be a lonely, solitary experience. Not so with a project like this, which would not have been completed without the support of numerous people. First, thank you to Dr. Mary Lou Shea, who improved my writing and encouraged me to keep moving forward (you know what I'm talking about!), and to Dr. Diane Leclerc, who provided invaluable editing and direction. This project would not be what it is without either of you. The Bible talks about iron sharpening iron; this book needed your sharpening! The gifts of personal investment and guidance from each of you are overwhelming.

Thank you also to my children, who made me a mother in the first place, and whose patient understanding gave me time for extra writing on top of a busy family schedule.

Finally, and primarily, this project would not have come to completion without the steadfast encouragement of my husband. The hours upon hours spent meticulously wading through text pale in comparison to the emotional support and additional parenting load he assumed throughout this process. Brian, thank you for being the kind of husband and father that resulted in my learning about unequal parenting the "easy way," through research but not personal life experience.

1

Mothers Today
How Did We Get Here?

"I REMEMBER WHEN I was doing a summer internship at a church," one middle-aged woman recalled. At the time of the internship, some years prior, she was a ministry major at a conservative Christian college, leading the teen group in a local church. Today, she was sitting in a church classroom, half of which was set up for preschoolers and the other half for adults, with coffee, fruit, and muffins on the counter. She was around the table with a handful of other women, all mothers, and the topic turned to mothering.

This woman continued, "One day, we were having a church picnic. I was single at the time and away from home but sitting with one of the church families. The father of that family couldn't make it that day, so it was just me, the mom, and the kids. I'm not sure why this mom started sharing with me, as I didn't know her well, but it was probably connected to my training to become a pastor. She said that when she was younger, she had thought she was called to ministry, too, just as I was. She followed this declaration of her pastoral calling with, 'but then I got married, and then . . .' and gestured to her children playing nearby. The implication was that she couldn't both have children and be a pastor; the former negated the possibility of the latter. She didn't admit it, but although she loved her children, her tone was a little regretful." This woman reflected, "I didn't know how to respond then, just as I didn't know how to respond about a year later when another woman in another church shared a similar story. This second woman had given up a career as a missionary for the same reason—she had gotten married and had children. She had the same love for her family and the same regretful tone. I wish I had had the wisdom to tell them it was not too late to follow God's call into ministry and that having a family didn't disqualify you. Sometimes, I wonder if they figured that out or if their lives as moms were too difficult to change once their kids were older.

"These experiences stuck with me and were part of why I attended seminary before having children; I was determined not to give up my calling and worried that children would interfere. It was probably also why I experienced such ambivalence when, after I had children, I decided to pastor only part-time. I wondered if I was giving up my calling, or part of it, in the way these women had. Having a family might not disqualify you from ministry, but I discovered there is a lot to be done and not enough time or energy to do it in. I couldn't do it all, although I wore myself out in trying. These were meaningful, essential years, but there were moments of breaking down out of exhaustion and being overwhelmed. There were times I was depressed. I constantly felt pulled in two directions, as if I should be a full-time pastor and a full-time, stay-at-home mom and excel at both simultaneously.

"Now I wonder why it was so important to me to 'do it all'—Why did I feel that everything had to fall on my shoulders? There were other options. However, even today, as I consider that, I realize I could never give up that time at home with my kids, as pressure-filled and stressful as it was. I guess I still feel that same ambivalence, even though those days are past."

While the details of this account may change, the outline is familiar to many. Another woman at the table, who had been in a position requiring extensive training and experience before becoming a mother, shared of her long list of mothering tasks: "It's hard because no 'one thing' is difficult; changing a single diaper is not difficult. Nothing requires high levels of skill or training, but put the list of responsibilities all together and it is overwhelming." The general idea behind her words was felt and affirmed by the other women, although there was some disagreement on the ease of changing a diaper. Squirmy toddlers and fathers who routinely "missed a spot," resulting in painful rashes for the diaper-wearer, were offered as evidence. It was agreed that although it was not always acknowledged, experience and skill had an impact on the quality of care. Another mom shared that mothers are expected to be everything at once—nutritionists, safety inspectors, professional cleaners, educators, psychologists, medical practitioners, child development experts, chauffeurs, etc.—so that while there are no special skills, training, or certifications either required or acknowledged, high levels of skills and expertise are needed. These skills and expertise are also often assumed to be innate to women who become mothers.

Yet another mom who had been listening quietly shared that she had only been in the area for a couple of years, having moved to be near her family after her divorce. As a single, working mother, she was trying to keep her head above water. She was thankful for her family's help but agreed that everyone looked to her regarding these expectations. When her children needed help or acted out, she was the one everyone looked to. She didn't have time to process others' opinions, but she did internalize them.

One among the group of mothers who could be considered a "super mom"—she grows much of her food, focuses on healthy eating, cooks meals for her family from scratch, homeschools her children, and has "hobbies" such as making honey or cheese—shared that she didn't know who she was outside of being a mother. "How would I spend my time if I didn't have to do all those things? What would I *like* to do? I don't even know." Her comments seemed to resonate with the group; a few added "mom identity" questions of their own.

The first mother shared again, revealing that when her children argue, she feels she has failed on three levels: (1) her kids were grumpy, meaning she failed to ensure they were content; (2) she failed to teach them how to interact with others when they were grumpy; and (3) her own response, which is often to scold, doesn't model the behavior she would like to see from them. Each of these women agreed that, in addition, mothers deal with the expectations that their children will behave perfectly and have happy, agreeable attitudes, both in front of others and at home. When they do not, the blame is placed on moms by others, by their own family members, and by themselves. These women also assume, as the pastoral candidate and her conversations reveal, that once a woman becomes a mother, the mother's role receives top priority.

These women, highly invested in their children and their responsibilities as mothers, affirm the general maxim that mothering is hard. The "institution" of motherhood, along with its ideals, expectations, and realities, is held up by today's society as a holy vocation, even as it is relegated to a second-class position. The act of mothering is demanding work, often leaving its practitioners drained and overwhelmed.[1] Conflicting messages

---

1. When used by this author, the term "motherhood" refers to the patriarchal institution that places restrictions on women as mothers. An example is described by Darcy

bombard today's mother, each voice claiming to share the correct approach to mothering. Many of these voices also share approaches to avoid, dividing mothers into "good" and "bad" categories (i.e., follow this approach to be a "good" mother, anyone who does not is a "bad" mother). While some relief might be expected to be found inside the support system of the Christian church, mothers within the Christian faith often experience the full impact of societal expectations and additional requirements added by church culture.

One unifying theme stands out among the mixed and conflicting messages: mothers are expected to meet and, if possible, exceed unrealistically high standards. Whatever else mothers' lives may entail, this is their top priority and their priority alone (fathers and other possible caregivers are exempt from these standards). Whatever a woman's identity was before she had children, now she is identified primarily as a "mom." How did our culture come to be this way? How can mothers make sense of the many messages insistent on dictating how they live? Where did these voices come from, what are their expectations, and how seriously should they be taken? American culture, including American evangelical church culture, implies that a "true woman" is a mother first, sacrificing all for her children and family. How does this compare with the foundational beliefs of the Christian faith? How does a Christian mother determine which voices to listen to, which to dismiss, and ultimately, where her identity lies?

COLONIAL AMERICA

It is enlightening to examine the origins of the motherhood messages found in current culture to be able to understand them. In the United States, mothers did not originally shoulder the responsibility to care for children at these high standards, nor to sort through the myriad voices promoting these standards. In fact, in colonial America, the voice of the fathers was the only voice mothers were obligated to listen to. The fathers, and not the mothers, were primarily responsible for their children. For "the

---

Lockman: "So-called moral motherhood is an ideology that vested moral authority in women as mothers but denied them political or economic authority. It was also child-centered, commanding women to put their children first and confining them to the home." Lockman, *All the Rage*, ch. 4. In contrast, "mothering" refers to the valuable and empowering act of care-work performed by mothers for their children and others, as coined by Adrienne Rich. Rich, *Of Woman Born*. Exceptions to these usages may be found in quotations from other authors.

nation's Puritan ancestors . . . mothers had no special place in the moral and spiritual education of their children. Fathers were considered the morally stronger of the two parents. . . . [She was not considered] as capable as a father of exercising the stern authority Puritan children were thought to require."[2] In contrast, women were thought to be too emotional, affectionate, and indulgent for that responsibility.[3] Additionally,

> The socialization of children was a widely shared task, certainly not reserved exclusively for, or even assigned primarily to, mothers. Because home and work were not separated for most colonial families, fathers and mothers were often present in children's day-to-day life. In families that could either afford servants or own slaves, these nonfamily members also shared in childcare. These servants or enslaved persons, therefore, had limited opportunities to spend time with their own children.[4]

While the work of parenting was shared, these women combined "the work of producing goods and services that provided food, shelter, and other material goods, with reproductive labor, the labor of bearing and rearing children, caring for the sick, and generally maintaining family life."[5]

THE REVOLUTIONARY PERIOD

This attitude shifted during the revolutionary period with the emergence of the "separate sphere" of home life apart from the rough and dirty world of "men's work" outside the home. This shift resulted in mothers who were charged with raising "virtuous sons who could continue to handle effectively the experiment of youthful self-government."[6] In other words, it was the mother's patriotic and moral duty to raise patriotic and moral sons. Now mothers, rather than fathers, were considered morally superior and responsible for maintaining virtue in the home and, by extension, the

---

2. Vandenberg-Daves, *Modern Motherhood*, 11.
3. Hays, *Cultural Contradictions*, 27.
4. Vandenberg-Daves, *Modern Motherhood*, 13. In an effort to acknowledge that the experience of white, middle-class mothers was not the whole of mothers' experiences in American history, references to the experiences of African American and Native American mothers, mothers who were enslaved, and mothers who were in domestic service are included. These references are not intended to be definitive; more work needs to be done in these and other areas of diversity among mothers.
5. Vandenberg-Daves, *Modern Motherhood*, 14–15.
6. Vandenberg-Daves, *Modern Motherhood*, 17–18.

nation. "In no time at all, this movement culminated in what has variously been called the 'cult of domesticity,' the 'cult of true womanhood,' and the 'Domestic Code': women, safely protected within the domestic enclave, would provide moral and emotional sustenance for their husbands and children and thereby participate in creating a more virtuous world."[7]

This grew stronger in the Victorian period. For mothers to act as the keepers of virtue, they needed to live lives of exemplary virtue themselves. It is during this era that "child rearing came to be understood as a task that was best done primarily by the individual mother—without reliance on servants, older children, or other women."[8] While this cultural shift elevated the role of the mother in some positive ways, it also required constant vigilance and self-sacrifice. These themes of vigilance and self-sacrifice have endured in cultural concepts of motherhood and prove to be some of the building blocks used to create the standards of motherhood today.

In contrast to this virtuous haven of home in which (white) women raised their children and avoided the outside world, "African American women's resourcefulness in providing for their children meant that their identities as providers necessarily contradicted the moral mother ideology. . . . African American women were breadwinners both during slavery and, for the vast majority, after slavery."[9] While "white Americans collectively fell in love with a mythological distortion of African American motherhood: the 'mammy' icon,"[10] the realities of life dictated that these mothers often relied on their community to help provide care for their children. "Most African American mothers also persisted in seeing their duties as a combination of materially providing for and emotionally nurturing children, while working with kin and community to do so. Their approach to mothering represented one of many real-world counterexamples to the ideal of a privatized nuclear family."[11]

Another counterexample to the privatized nuclear family, and the established motherhood ideal of the time, was revealed in the practice of separating Indigenous children from their families, an instance in which it

---

7. Hays, *Cultural Contradictions*, 30.
8. Hays, *Cultural Contradictions*, 32.
9. Vandenberg-Daves, *Modern Motherhood*, 38. For a description of mothering among slaves, including descriptions of "forced" motherhood by slave owners, see Leclerc, "'Purified Through Fire,'" 110–27.
10. Vandenberg-Daves, *Modern Motherhood*, 42.
11. Vandenberg-Daves, *Modern Motherhood*, 39.

was often mothers who were blamed for instigating trauma on the families of others. "It was mostly the women's domain in the colonial project to dispossess—or separate—children from their Indigenous, biological mothers in the name of 'civilizing' the children. Hence, many white Christian mothers harmed Indigenous people by directly targeting the most intimate of human bonds: that of mother and child."[12] Ironically, it was the elevation of the motherhood role that, paired with racism, resulted in mothers committing this atrocity against mothers and their children. Similar race-based atrocities may otherwise have occurred without this rise in motherhood status. However, in this instance, cultural differences in mothering practices were highlighted because of mothers' newly realized roles as keepers of virtue and "civilization." The highlighting of these differences perpetuated this unvirtuous, uncivilized tragedy.

SCIENTIFIC MOTHERHOOD

The end of the nineteenth century brought another shift in perceptions of motherhood, as scientific advances filtered into the mother–child dynamic. The medical community established itself as the authority in the proper care of infants and children, instilling rigid standards of hygiene, scheduling, and feeding in middle-class homes. "Scientific motherhood increasingly cast mothers as compliant consumers of expertise in arenas once controlled by women."[13] While this scientific progress did often improve health and legitimated mothers' work to a degree, it also created an atmosphere of judgment for those who did not live up to scientific standards.[14] "All this emphasis on scientific methods in child rearing was accompanied by a more general surge in the importance attached to children."[15] This increased understanding of children's importance and the new expectations that mothers seek and follow the experts' advice added to the themes of mothers' vigilance, piety, and self-sacrifice.

These expectations were, for this time, largely limited to white, middle-class families. Women of color instead "were very often confined to low-paying domestic service positions in the homes of white families,"[16]

---

12. Marga, *Image of Her*, 148.
13. Vandenberg-Daves, *Modern Motherhood*, 85.
14. Vandenberg-Daves, *Modern Motherhood*, 90.
15. Hays, *Cultural Contradictions*, 41.
16. Vandenberg-Daves, *Modern Motherhood*, 108.

and Native American mothers in particular "were not seen as up to the task of accomplishing modernization themselves."[17] The Bureau of Indian Affairs continued to remove children from the home to break up families and "assimilate" children to white culture.[18] It is clear that at this point in history, the motherhood ideal that insists a mother remain at home with her children only extended so far.

By the 1940s, the field of science had progressed to include psychology, and with it the emergence of a new form of judgment was layered on top of perceptions of motherhood. Mothers now had the additional responsibility to raise happy, productive, well-adjusted children into adulthood. Any perceived deviance from this path, such as children who were unhappy or otherwise nonproductive members of society, was laid at the feet of the mother. "A deeply psychologized and malicious form of mother blame emerged . . . [vesting mothers] with a sinister mission: depriving sons of their rightful masculinity through controlling and even monstrous mother-love."[19] Now mothers needed to be ever-vigilant, self-sacrificing, able to research and apply expert scientific advice and recognize the heightened importance of each child, all while maintaining the appropriate emotional distance so as not to damage their children psychologically.

INTENSIVE MOTHERING

New childcare manuals now emerged, detailing exactly how parents (mothers) are to achieve these goals. Sharon Hays summarizes what she has coined "intensive mothering" as prescribed by some of these early manuals:

> First, they assume that child care is primarily the responsibility of the individual mother. Second, the methods they recommend are child-centered, expert-guided, emotionally absorbing, labor-intensive, and financially expensive. Finally, they clearly treat the child as . . . sacred, innocent, and pure, their price immeasurable, and decisions regarding their rearing completely distinct from questions of efficiency or financial profitability.[20]

---

17. Vandenberg-Daves, *Modern Motherhood*, 116.
18. Vandenberg-Daves, *Modern Motherhood*, 115.
19. Vandenberg-Daves, *Modern Motherhood*, 177.
20. Hays, *Cultural Contradictions*, 54.

While not all experts espoused the "permissive parenting" promoted by several of these manuals, they all reinforced the ideology of intensive mothering. For example, Dr. James Dobson, and his book *Dare to Discipline*, "attacks permissive child rearing, urges greater strictness, advises parents to shape their child's will, and suggests that they seek guidance from God and the Bible."[21] Although Dobson did not promote permissive parenting as other childcare manuals did, he still promoted intensive parenting in that he encouraged parents to center family life on what is best for the child, with detailed information on how to accomplish this. A proliferation of parenting books written in more recent years reinforces this perspective, regardless of the approach advocated by their authors. Examples of these parenting approaches include, but are not limited to, attachment parenting, free-range parenting, and gentle parenting.

Previous cultural shifts in perceptions of motherhood excluded those who were not middle-class and white. Now, although differences between people groups are noted, they "should not obscure their common recognition of the larger ideology of intensive child rearing and their shared commitment to good mothering . . . [these differences] do not pose a serious challenge to the dominance of the ideology of intensive mothering."[22] This perspective has proven resilient; "the ideology of intensive mothering persisted. It survived Betty Freidan's (1963) famous attack on the 'feminine mystique,'" concern over psychological missteps by mothers, pushback over permissive parenting (primarily as taught by Dr. Spock), and "feminism's 'second wave' of activism, which included the proliferation of literature damning the family as an oppressive institution. Indeed, the ideology of intensive mothering has only grown more extensive and elaborate in the present day."[23] The motivation behind this seems to be that although this type of intensive parenting may be complex, it is worth whatever it costs to put children first.

The ideology of intensive mothering mirrors what Susan Douglas and Meredith Michaels have termed the "new momism," defined as "the insistence that no woman is truly complete or fulfilled unless she has kids, that women remain the best primary caretakers of children, and that to be a remotely decent mother, a woman has to devote her entire physical,

---

21. Hays, *Cultural Contradictions*, 69.
22. Hays, *Cultural Contradictions*, 94–95.
23. Hays, *Cultural Contradictions*, 50.

psychological, emotional, and intellectual being, 24/7, to her children."[24] As does Hays, these authors contend that this philosophy has survived and even grown throughout the various shifts in cultural perceptions of motherhood, going so far as to state, "The new momism is the direct descendant and latest version of what Betty Friedan famously labeled the 'feminine mystique' back in the 1960s."[25]

MEDIA INFLUENCE

No overview of the voices speaking into the lives of mothers today would be complete without looking at the media, which is precisely what Douglas and Michaels do:

> There have been, since the early 1980s, several overlapping media frameworks that have fueled the new momism. First, the media warned mothers about the external threats to their kids from abductors and the like. Then the "family values" crowd made it clear that supporting the family was not part of the government's responsibility. By the late 1980s, stories about welfare and crack mothers emphasized the internal threats to children from mothers themselves.[26]

Mothers are now required to be not only vigilant, self-sacrificing, scientific, and psychological experts, recognizing the high value of placing children first, but they must also be constantly on the alert for would-be kidnappers or abusers.[27] Additionally, the racial divide again appears as African American women are repeatedly (and inaccurately) pictured in the news as the "bad" mothers on welfare and crack.[28]

---

24. Douglas and Michaels, *Mommy Myth*, intro.
25. Douglas and Michaels, *Mommy Myth*, intro.
26. Douglas and Michaels, *Mommy Myth*, intro.

27. While the news media reported actual, alleged cases of abductions and abuse, the sensationalized depictions portrayed the risk of these awful events occurring higher than they were. "Wildly exaggerated figures—that as many as two million kids disappeared each year and that five thousand a year were abducted and killed—circulated in the media. Revised figures in 1988 suggested that, in fact, somewhere between two and three hundred kids nationally were abducted by strangers for any length of time." Further, some of the abuse allegations, such as in the famous McMartin case, were false. Nevertheless, the false accusations received wide publicity, while the "not guilty" verdict did not. Douglas and Michaels, *Mommy Myth*, ch. 3.

28. For a fuller discussion on this trend, see Douglas and Michaels, *Mommy Myth*, chs. 5 and 6.

The media added another dimension to contemporary motherhood with the invention of the "mommy wars." In this narrative, moms who work outside the home,

> Regularly describe stay-at-home mothers as lazy and boring, while traditional moms regularly accuse employed mothers of selfishly neglecting their children.
>
> This portrait of the mommy wars is both exaggerated and superficial. In fact, the majority of mothers . . . expressed respect for one another's need or right to choose whether to go out to work or stay at home with the kids. . . . They also share a whole set of similar concerns regarding appropriate child rearing.[29]

Further, "millions of mothers move between these two categories, have been one and then the other at various different times, creating a mosaic of work and child-rearing practices that bears no resemblance to the supposed ironclad roles suggested by the 'mommy wars.'"[30]

Another fascinating media portrayal of mothers was first presented by the *New York Times* in 2003 in an article titled "The Opt-Out Revolution."[31] The article begins with a gathering of eight Princeton graduates who each "opted out" of their established careers to stay at home with their children. These mothers were presented as representative of an entire group of high-achieving women who decided the cost of careers was too high compared to staying home to raise their children. Other media coverage included "a Time magazine cover story on 'The Case for Staying Home' and a '60 Minutes' segment devoted to a group of former mega-achievers who were, as the anchor Lesley Stahl put it, 'giving up money, success and big futures' to be home with their children."[32] This supposed trend seemed to claim that feminism did not "work" after all; women belonged in the home with their children and were choosing that path even when they had other options. However, "Ninety-three percent of those who leave work to parent intend to return to their careers, and the average amount of time that women take away from their careers is 2.2 years. The college students I meet have their lives planned out exactly this way—career in their twenties, babies in their thirties. It's not babies in exchange for a career, but one and then

---

29. Hays, *Cultural Contradictions*, 132.
30. Douglas and Michaels, *Mommy Myth*, intro.
31. Belkin, "Opt-Out Revolution."
32. Warner, "Opt-Out Generation Wants Back."

the other."³³ Follow-up articles on the Opt-Out Revolution confirmed this trend; those who opted out in 2003 were now returning to jobs and careers with varying levels of success.³⁴

Amid the ambivalence of the "mommy wars" or "opting out," and in contrast to the negative depictions of drug-addicted welfare moms, the idealized mother was personified in the celebrity mom.³⁵ These mothers were portrayed as happily devoted to their children, offering them the best they had to offer, including whatever their considerable means and influence could buy. These women openly shared that their children were more valuable to them than their careers, even though it was their professional success that earned them spots on magazine covers:

> The celebrity mom profile, while presenting images of working mothers who had allegedly found a balance between work and family, was a powerful Trojan horse, reinforcing all of the tenets of the new momism, and particularly intensive mothering, at a time when mothers were working harder than ever. And most important, the message of the celebrity mom profile has evolved from "how I do it all" to "it's really much more fun and rewarding to quit my job and stay home with the kids."³⁶

The not-so-subtle message became that "those of us who 'chose' to work full-time (and even overtime) because we have to, want to, or both, are, in this Hollywood-dictated family album, selfish mothers with absolutely wrong priorities."³⁷

In addition to those featured in women's magazines and on televised morning shows, a new kind of celebrity mom emerged "between roughly 2005 and 2010 . . . the first wave of mommy bloggers, who wrote confessional,

---

33. Richards, *Opting In*, ch. 1.

34. Warner, "Opt-Out Generation Wants Back."

35. Described negatively by Philip Wylie in his book *Generation of Vipers*, "mom" was originally a derogatory term compared to the admirable term "mother." "Momism" was thus defined as a psychologically damaging approach to motherhood. However, as suggested by its use here in the phrase "celebrity mom," the term "mom" has evolved to suggest a positive, "get real" designation that is more relaxed than the formal "mother." Other common uses include, but are not limited to, "soccer mom," "dance mom," or "stay-at-home mom" (SAHM). A quick internet search for "mom gear," where the term has been commercialized in abundance, confirms the trend of the positive usage of this term.

36. Douglas and Michaels, *Mommy Myth*, ch. 4.

37. Douglas and Michaels, *Mommy Myth*, ch. 4.

raw accounts of their experiences on amateur blogs. . . . The mommy bloggers were the first media voices who spoke directly—and exclusively—to mothers."[38] Eventually, these blogs turned to more visual formats such as Instagram and, "'When blogs went visual, we saw the beginning of [commercialization] . . . people began to see they could make more money with aspirational content—because brands prefer it. Aspirational sells better than truth-telling.' . . . As online motherhood shifted from uncensored to aspirational, many mommy blogs became 'lifestyle' blogs, and bloggers became influencers."[39] These "mommy influencers" "broadcast a clean and chipper vision of motherhood, replete with D. I. Y. crafting projects and coordinated family photo shoots. . . . This saintly moment might be the most demanding iteration of motherhood since the Victorian era."[40]

A brief overview of today's mommy influencers showcases women of color, women of various body types, moms of multiples, working moms, SAHMs, single moms, and married moms. They address addiction, depression, holistic living, infertility, fitness, crafting, healthy eating, spirituality, fashion, self-care, travel, home design, blended families, and more, often with a humorous twist.[41] We have moved beyond magazines, television, blogs, and even websites. "Today's most popular representations of motherhood aren't necessarily occurring on websites anymore, but rather through multi-platform personal brands. . . . They're profane and genuinely self-deprecating, but glossier and more aspirational than mothers have ever been."[42] These aspirations now encompass every mother in every niche. In addition to the expectations of being constantly alert and perfectly raising perfect children, mothers need to add D. I. Y. projects, professionally staged homes, a sharp wit, and spontaneous but beautifully photographed family lives to their list of expectations (or at least look like they do). They also need to do all of this with an aura of authenticity; whether or not they are, they need to look like they are "keeping it real."

38. Jezer-Morton, "Did Moms Exist Before."
39. Jezer-Morton, "Did Moms Exist Before."
40. Jezer-Morton, "Did Moms Exist Before."
41. Boyd and Pomarico, "30 Mommy Influencers."
42. Jezer-Morton, "Did Moms Exist Before."

MOTHERS TODAY

Mothers today inherit many layers of expectations depicting how a "good" mother raises her children. At the same time, second-wave feminism and the women's movement of the 1960s and 1970s did change cultural perspectives on women in the workplace. It is generally no longer the case that women are confined to the sphere of the home, avoiding the working world outside the home as the exclusive sphere of men. While fifty to sixty years ago the debate centered around whether it was acceptable for mothers to engage in paid work outside the home, and both the "mommy wars" and the "opt-out revolution" attempted to reignite that debate, the question seems to have been answered, in action if not in rhetoric. Women (including moms) work.[43] However, this does not mean the layers of motherhood expectations are exchanged for a career. "Post-feminism means that you can now work outside the home even in jobs previously restricted to men, go to graduate school, pump iron, and pump your own gas, as long as you remain fashion conscious, slim, nurturing, deferential to men, and become a doting, selfless mother."[44]

With the addition of careers and impossibly high standards for what it takes to be a "good" mother, who is making all of this happen?

> The most recent time-use diary information collected by Pew Research and the Bureau of Labor Statistics in the U.S. consistently finds that women who work outside of the home shoulder 65 percent of child care responsibilities, and their male partners 35 percent. Those percentages have held steady since the year 2000. In the last twenty years, that figure has not budged.[45]

From where do these hours come? "Mothers maintain their child care time almost regardless of their employment obligations. They accomplish this by cutting back on leisure time, personal care, and sleep. This hardly varies by race or ethnicity."[46] Often, mothers wear this lack of self-care as a badge of honor as they scramble to care for everyone and everything

---

43. The Bureau of Labor Statistics reports that there are even more women in the workforce than men at times. In December 2019, women held 50.04 percent of jobs. In addition, during the Great Recession, women held more jobs than men between June 2009 and April 2010. "For the first time in nearly a decade, women held more jobs than men." See USAFACTS, "Labor Force."

44. Douglas and Michaels, *Mommy Myth*, intro.

45. Lockman, *All the Rage*, intro.

46. Lockman, *All the Rage*, ch. 1.

else in their realm of responsibility, upholding the standards of intensive, influencer-style mothering. It seems "mothering . . . is a task evaluated not only by outcomes (the general health and happiness of children) but also by how much deprivation a woman is willing to endure. Self-denial as a virtue; self-flagellation as a rule."[47]

Beyond balancing a career with childcare, "even when mothers earn more, an increasingly common phenomenon, couples tend to decide that it should be she, rather than he, who becomes the secondary breadwinner. It is disproportionately women who forgo economic security and well-being when they become parents."[48] This phenomenon was drastically highlighted when the pandemic of 2020 hit, instigating "on-again, off-again school and day care closures around the world," clarifying that "there's not a doubt as to who has borne the brunt of the caregiving burden: mothers. . . . As a result, millions of women—particularly those with children—were either pushed out of their jobs or were forced to downsize their careers, spurring what many economists are calling the world's first 'she-cession.'"[49] The February 2022 Jobs Report reflects, "Women now make up more than two in three (68.5%) net job losers since the start of this crisis. . . . This brings the total number of women who have left the labor force since February 2020 to over 1.1 million. By comparison, 479,000 men ages 20 and over entered the labor force last month. This means women now make up all labor force leavers since February 2020."[50]

Even when women retain their higher-earning jobs, influence in the domestic sphere does not follow their more significant income. "Rather than using their earning power to balance any scales, high-earning wives chose to demur to masculine prerogatives. The rising status of women outside the home has actually increased our inclination to reinforce male dominance inside it."[51] Mothers who work for pay outside the home compensate by not only deferring to male prerogative but also by going to great lengths to "approximate the at-home mother."[52] Regardless of their employment status and other possible demands on their time, the expectation is set

---

47. Lockman, *All the Rage*, ch. 5.
48. Lockman, *All the Rage*, ch. 1.
49. Gupta, "Covid Shuttered Schools Everywhere."
50. National Women's Law Center, "Jobs Report." This article cites numerous factors, in addition to childcare, involved in women leaving the labor force.
51. Lockman, *All the Rage*, ch. 3.
52. Lockman, *All the Rage*, ch. 5.

that mothers, not fathers, will achieve and maintain high levels of intensive parenting. Women "are no longer demonized for working. In exchange, we prostrate ourselves before our children for all the world to see."[53]

Today's ideologies and motherhood practices allow for careers while simultaneously raising the bar around intensive mothering. However, they also mirror the past in many ways. These ideologies and practices stem from American culture at large. While they claim to promote a more egalitarian stance than in the past, "Either mothers are individual women with the same constitutional and personal rights to freedom and self-development as any other human being or they are less than fully autonomous beings, mere adjuncts to children and others."[54] This surprising conclusion concedes that although culture may have progressed to be more egalitarian in theory, "Conventions embodying male dominance have changed much less in 'the personal' than in the job world. . . . If you get down to it, we talk about equality, but the part people grasped on to was women changing. Women can have careers, be in the military, become clergy. But the fact is that all of that doesn't work if household stuff doesn't shift. And some things are more impervious to change than others."[55] In actual practice, if not in ideology, contemporary culture mirrors the religious view of complementarianism espoused by portions of the Christian community.

COMPLEMENTARIANISM

Complementarianism adds another voice speaking into the expectations of motherhood, especially for those mothers in the evangelical church. In short, complementarianism is a viewpoint claiming that men and women are mandated different but complementary roles in biblical texts. The prescribed role for men is to lead and the prescribed role for women is to follow men's leadership, especially as wives and mothers. The statement defining complementarianism, approved at the June 1998 Southern Baptist Convention, claims, "A wife is to submit herself graciously to the servant leadership of her husband even as the church willingly submits to the headship of Christ. She, being in the image of God as is her husband and thus equal to

---

53. Lockman, *All the Rage*, ch. 5.
54. Douglas and Michaels, *Mommy Myth*, ch. 2.
55. Lockman, *All the Rage*, ch. 1.

him, has the God-given responsibility to respect her husband and to serve as his helper in managing the household and nurturing the next generation."[56]

What does complementarian ideology intend by instructing wives to submit to their husbands? Grudem and Piper explain that this is understood, "not in terms of specific behaviors, but as a disposition to yield to the husband's authority and an inclination to follow his leadership."[57] They further expand, "In a well-ordered biblical marriage both husband and wife acknowledge in principle that, if necessary in some disagreement, the husband will accept the burden of making the final choice."[58] Ephesians 5:21–33 is often cited in connection with this principle, especially verses 22–23 and 33: "Wives, be subject to your husbands as you are to the Lord. For the husband is the head of the wife" and "a wife should respect her husband." Although it is often used to do so, this does not connote inferiority or the kind of complementarian submission prescribed above. "Yes, wives are to submit, but so are husbands. Instead of underscoring the inferiority of women, Ephesians 5 underscores the equality of women—they are called to submit in verse 22, just like their husbands are called to submit in verse 21. . . . The mutual submission in verse 21 'is characteristic of a way of life that sets believers apart from the nonbelieving world."[59] C. S. Cowles asks,

> Precisely, how does Christ exercise His headship over the Church, and thus the husband exercise his headship over his wife? Paul's answer is, "Christ *loved* the church and *gave himself up for her*" (5:25, emphasis added). The authority that Christ exercises over His Church as its head is not like that of the Gentiles. To the contrary . . . "the Son of Man came not to be served but to serve, and to give his life a ransom for many" (Mark 10:45). In other words, Christ turns the world's (Gentile's) understanding of *arche* headship right on its head. He speaks not of *arche*-ship (rulership) but of *kephale*-ship (servanthood) and in doing so destroys the fundamental assumptions of patriarchalism.[60]

This reversal in understanding is underscored by Barr's comment on Paul's writing: "Instead of focusing on wifely submission (everyone was doing that), the Christian household codes demand that the husband do exactly

---

56. Barr, *Making of Biblical Womanhood*, 19.
57. Piper and Grudem, *Recovering Biblical Manhood*, 55.
58. Piper and Grudem, *Recovering Biblical Manhood*, 47.
59. Barr, *Making of Biblical Womanhood*, 50.
60. Cowles, *Woman's Place?*, 123–24.

the opposite of what Roman law allowed: sacrificing his life for his wife instead of exercising power over her life."[61]

Colossians 3:18—"Wives, be subject to your husbands, as is fitting in the Lord"—is another Scripture used to support the complementarian theme of wifely submission. However, "in Colossians 3, Paul opens his discussion of the household with a call to *wives first*—not to the man presumably in charge.... Paul emphasizes that wives should be subject as *fitting in the Lord* (not because they are inferior) and that husbands should love their wives.... Jesus, not the Roman paterfamilias, is in charge of the Christian household."[62] Likewise, in today's context, it is Jesus, not the complementarian husband, in charge of the Christian household.

The complementarian approach to these passages and others like them seems to focus on the question, "Who is *really* in charge? Who has the final authority?" Regardless of the call for men to *servant* leadership when they accept the "burden of making the final choice,"[63] attempting to define "who is in charge" misses the point, not only of these passages but also of the gospel itself. These verses are not about authority. They are not asking, "Who is in charge?" or "Who is the decision-maker?" but rather, "Who can love the other? Who is laying down their life (and authority) for the other?" As with the example Jesus set when washing his disciples' feet, husbands and wives are entreated to love and serve each other, both called to mutual submission. Jesus chose to act as the servant in John 13. He not only chose to perform the lowly work of foot-washing, but also placed himself in a powerless position. Jesus was not doing the work of foot-washing while simultaneously maintaining authority; instead, he was entering the subordinate role of the servant. This act was intended as more than a one-time event, which is apparent when Jesus stated, "For I have set you an example, that you also should do as I have done to you" (John 13:15). That this was

---

61. Barr, *Making of Biblical Womanhood*, 55.

62. Barr, *Making of Biblical Womanhood*, 49–50.

63. Automatically assigning final decision-making in cases of a disagreement to one person in a marriage relationship undercuts the relationship itself, depriving the married couple of developing skills to "work it out" in a loving partnership. In contrast, pursuing problem-solving and conflict-management tools can draw a couple closer, deepening their relationship. It encourages both the relationship and the individuals to mature. It also allows space for both spouses to be authentically themselves, doing away with the requirement to repress honest thoughts, desires, and knowledge. This space for authenticity, in turn, opens the door to spouses truly knowing each other (intimacy). This approach simultaneously helps couples "share the load." Shared decision-making enables shared responsibility.

not out of character is demonstrated again when he submits completely to earthly authority and allows himself to be crucified. This intentional subordination is how Jesus was the "head of the church" and how husbands are to be "the head of the wife," not by insisting on authority but instead by participating in mutual submission. That husbands were explicitly addressed on this issue, rather than only wives, demonstrates the countercultural nature of the passage:

> The only hierarchy that fits within Kingdom relationships is where the first continually seek to be the last and the least. . . . Husbands and wives, men and women are to live together—not under the rule of law but within the reign of grace. The proper paradigm for relating to one another "in Christ" is not that of a king sitting high upon his throne but that of a servant bowed low with a towel about his waist and a wash basin in his hands.[64]

Rather than following this example themselves, many men instead delegate this role to their wives, especially those wives who are also mothers.[65]

Alongside the expectations to submit to their husbands, the complementarian statement above relegates women to the "helper" role. The reasoning behind this statement is inaccurately pulled from the creation account found in Genesis, specifically Gen 2:18 which states, "The LORD God said, 'It is not good that the man should be alone; I will make him a helper as his partner.'" Piper and Grudem explain that "God teaches us that the woman is a man's 'helper' in the sense of a loyal and suitable assistant in the life of the garden."[66] Women then are not equal partners but rather subordinate "assistants." As long as women are assistants rather than partners, patriarchal male prerogative will remain intact; women will continue to be expected to work harder and longer and men will feel no obligation to participate. As the designated, submissive "helper," parenting will remain primarily women's work. The result is that motherhood is not only ingrained with the hyper-expectations of today's intensive mothering, but it has now also been relegated to "assistant" status. Consequently, mothers are expected to maintain high levels of parenting with all the responsibility but none of the authority, expected to follow the headship of someone who is minimally involved. Is the complementarian interpretation of this Genesis

---

64. Cowles, *Woman's Place?*, 126.

65. For a discussion on the Household Rules found in Col 3:18–4:1; Titus 2:1–10; and 1 Pet 3:1–7, see Orjala Serrão, "Challenging Passages," 62–64.

66. Piper and Grudem, *Recovering Biblical Manhood*, 108.

passage accurate? A closer look at the original language of this passage reveals, "English versions consistently translate *'ezer* as 'helper,'" although,

> We must avoid the English connotation of someone of inferior status or skill.
>
> In the Hebrew Scriptures, "helper" means just the opposite. When the Bible speaks of a helper, it usually refers to God the Helper, the Rescuer of those who cannot help themselves. If *'ezer* should be translated "helper" here, it means God intended to make someone who would rescue the *'adam* [human person] from solitude. This would be God's final step in making a creature in God's own image, which includes living intimately in community.[67]

However, "in some passages *'ezer* . . . means 'helper,' but in other passages *'ezer* . . . means 'strength,' or 'power.'"[68] In determining which translation is most accurate, it is helpful to notice the word following *'ezer* in the original text, which is *cenegdo*. The definition of *cenegdo* is a combination, partially meaning "'like,' 'as,' 'according to.' This being . . . [would be] of the same kind or species. This one, too, would be *'adam*.'"[69] This is combined with the meaning, "'facing,' in the sense of standing in one's presence as an equal and other entity . . . [who] by their position and by their body language, acknowledge each other as equals."[70] Taken together,

> A straightforward literal translation is, "I will make for it a power like [it], facing it." An expansive paraphrase, expressing in English all the Hebrew intends, might read, "To end the loneliness of the single human, I will make another power, another autonomous being, like it, corresponding to it, of the same species, and facing it, standing opposite it in an equal I-Thou relationship, another human, its equal. And when I have finished that last creative step, the human species will be both male and female."[71]

Notice there is no hint of one person taking the lead, expecting to be followed by the other who has been designated the "assistant." Woman, then, is not the weaker creation, destined to follow man's lead. Although there are different genders, gender roles are not assigned. "The advent of sexual characteristics does not imply inequality and subordination, but evolves

---

67. Coleson, *Ezer Cenegdo*, 11–12.
68. Coleson, *Ezer Cenegdo*, 13.
69. Coleson, *Ezer Cenegdo*, 13.
70. Coleson, *Ezer Cenegdo*, 13.
71. Coleson, *Ezer Cenegdo*, 14.

out of the goodness of creation (Gen 1:31) and the necessity for human relationality at the core of human existence. It is not good to 'be alone.'"[72] Man and woman rescue each other from solitude, living and working together as equal partners.

According to the defining complementarian statement above, a woman as the helper is given the responsibility by God "to manage the household and nurture the next generation."[73] Piper and Grudem further detail that "supporting the family is primarily the responsibility of the husband. Caring for the children is primarily the responsibility of the wife."[74] They view these roles as part of the created order, again returning to the creation account in Genesis, claiming this is how God intended men and women to interact from the beginning. In this viewpoint, to contradict complementarianism is to contradict God's intent for humankind and the created order. "The point of this Genesis text . . . does suggest that any role reversal at these basic levels of child care and breadwinning labor will be contrary to the original intention of God, and contrary to the way he made us as male and female for our ordained roles."[75]

Although the complementarian claim is that men and women are charged with different roles and responsibilities from the beginning, the actual creation account found in Genesis fails to bear this out. When reading Gen 1:26–28, the passage where God creates humankind in God's image (male and female!), then says to them, "Be fruitful and multiply, and fill the earth and subdue it; and have dominion over the fish of the sea and over the birds of the air and over every living thing that moves upon the earth."

> It is helpful to notice that both genders are named explicitly in this context of dominion-giving and commissioning. Unless by willful ignorance, no one could read these verses and conclude that *only men* are in charge. . . . This shared leadership over creation is even more apparent in the Hebrew text, where every pronoun and command takes plural form.[76]

Not only are both male and female charged with this leadership, "The story arc of Eden highlights the reality that the human task of dominion *cannot be completed* only by men . . . the first pair become a pair precisely

---

72. Miller-McLemore, *Also a Mother*, 140.
73. Barr, *Making of Biblical Womanhood*, 19.
74. Piper and Grudem, *Recovering Biblical Manhood*, 50.
75. Piper and Grudem, *Recovering Biblical Manhood*, 50.
76. Derck, "Old Testament," 72–73.

so that both can exercise stewardship over Eden."⁷⁷ There is no hint that specific gender roles are assigned; instead, both genders are instructed to share in the responsibilities to be fruitful, multiply, fill, subdue, and have dominion over the earth. One gender is not more or less responsible for any of these charges than the other. We are reminded that man and woman rescue each other from solitude, living and working together as equal partners. "Complementarians may argue that women are equal to men. . . . Yet their insistence that 'equal worth' manifests in unequal roles refutes this."⁷⁸ In the same vein, secular society's insistence that egalitarianism manifests in unequal workloads refutes claims of egalitarianism.

The complementarian insistence that women's role be restricted to caring for children and homes extends beyond proof-texting biblical passages and into claims about biology. "Females have been concerned more heavily with infant care due to breast feeding,⁷⁹ and males with provision of food. In support of this basic division of labor, God has given each sex special gifts to carry out its task."⁸⁰ These "special gifts" purportedly include "female-infant bonding,"⁸¹ higher emotional intelligence,⁸² and a "more responsive sensory system [that] allows them to monitor their environment more completely and with more discrimination."⁸³ "By virtue of their gifts in language, their more networked nervous system, their acuity of perception, and their patience, women are more comfortable with and gravitate to social interaction and communication. They have physiologies and temperament traits that prepare them uniquely for child care. Their maternal instincts and bonding facility are stronger."⁸⁴ This argument finds a counterpart in society at large.

---

77. Derck, "Old Testament," 73–74 (emphasis in original).

78. Barr, *Making of Biblical Womanhood*, 18.

79. It is important to note that while women have the singular ability to breastfeed and men do not, this is no longer the only way to feed an infant, nor has it been for decades. Further, the length of time an infant needs to be fed exclusively by either breast or bottle is short; it is a matter of months. While feeding a child is inarguably essential, it is also hardly the only necessary task involved in infant care and childcare. Breastfeeding does not give women a monopoly on the physical ability to care for infants.

80. Piper and Grudem, *Recovering Biblical Manhood*, 358.

81. Piper and Grudem, *Recovering Biblical Manhood*, 360.

82. Piper and Grudem, *Recovering Biblical Manhood*, 357.

83. Piper and Grudem, *Recovering Biblical Manhood*, 357.

84. Piper and Grudem, *Recovering Biblical Manhood*, 367. In contrast, "The more lateralized male brain would be expected to be more single-minded, focused, less

BIOLOGY

Research shows the majority of Americans "deem women the de facto presumptive better match for each and every kid-related task. . . . In 2016, Pew Research found that breastfeeding aside, 53 percent of adults say that a mother is better equipped than a father to care for children (1 percent said a father is better; 45 percent that the two are equal)."[85] Further, "Myths about innate maternal love convey the message that men are somehow ill-equipped to share the responsibility of child rearing, lacking some physiological love that only mothers have."[86] These beliefs assume biological gender differences and further reinforce separate roles for men and women, explicitly assigning women as primary caretakers of children. It is important to note that there is a strong, culturally conditioned foundation for this. "We derive our belief that primary maternal care is natural, inborn, and obvious from a long history of female subjugation. We call that history 'nature' and continue to surmise that the sex bearing children must provide them with most of their care. Sciencey-sounding terms like 'maternal instinct,' which have no paternal equivalent, reinforce that thinking."[87] At times, the scientific world has used its influence to back these beliefs up. However,

> In 2005, Hyde rounded up forty-six meta-analyses of gender difference studies whose domains included cognitive abilities, communication, social behavior, personality, and psychological well-being, to name a handful. Her goal was to determine the effect size, or statistical strength, of the variables in question. . . . For 78 percent of the gender differences measured and remeasured and measured once again, there was actually as much of a difference within gender as between gender. Differences between two women or two men were at least as likely as differences between any female/male pair.[88]

"Based on the findings of her meta-analysis, Hyde proposed 'the gender similarities hypothesis,' which asserts that, distinctive reproductive systems

---

distractible, and perhaps less socially aware. This, coupled with the hot-wired limbic system, may increase males' competitive, goal-setting, rule-making, hierarchical approach to social interaction." Piper and Grudem, *Recovering Biblical Manhood*, 364.

85. Lockman, *All the Rage*, ch. 2.
86. Miller-McLemore, *Also a Mother*, 164.
87. Lockman, *All the Rage*, ch. 2.
88. Lockman, *All the Rage*, ch. 2.

aside, men and women are similar in more ways than not."[89] At the most basic level, "the male brain is like nothing in the world so much as a female brain. Neuroscientists can't even tell them apart at an individual level."[90] This carries over into childbearing and childcaring as well. While there are undoubtedly physical changes in women as they gestate, men mirror many of these changes in preparation for parenthood:

> Throughout the prenatal period, men in close contact with pregnant partners are physiologically primed to care for infants. Expectant fathers experience a rise in the levels of the pregnancy-related hormones prolactin, cortisol, and estrogen in proportion to that of their baby's mother. Additionally, testosterone, associated with competition for mates, declines. Second-time fathers produce even more prolactin and less testosterone in the company of a pregnant partner than do first-timers.[91]

This mirroring phenomenon does not disappear once the pregnancy ends and a child is born, as "involved fathers continue to experience hormonal changes. In North America, men in long-term relationships like marriage and fatherhood almost uniformly have lower testosterone levels than their single and childless counterparts."[92] This suggests that presumed biological differences are much less significant than the complementarian community and, indeed, the general public believes.

How has American secular society, which presumably does not share the religious beliefs of the complementarian subculture, come to have such strong beliefs about gender roles, specifically that of motherhood? Practically speaking, with the understanding that even at the biological level, men and women are more alike than they are different, how have women come to be considered the most qualified primary caretakers?

> Psychologist Ross Parke and colleagues studied fathers of newborns in maternity wards. For most of the behaviors his team measured, fathers and mothers hardly differed. Men spoke to babies in high-pitched voices and responded with sensitivity to infant cues during feeding. They also exhibited patterns similar to their wives in heart rate, blood pressure, and skin conductance when holding their children. The major difference Parke observed was that

---

89. Lockman, *All the Rage*, ch. 2.
90. Lockman, *All the Rage*, ch. 2.
91. Lockman, *All the Rage*, ch. 2.
92. Lockman, *All the Rage*, ch. 2.

fathers, unlike mothers, took a step back from their child's care in the presence of their spouse. Their assumption that a baby primarily needs his mother limited their involvement.[93]

This assumption becomes a self-fulfilling prophecy as what begins in the maternity wards continues forward, becoming part of parents' newly established routines. "When one parent gets into the habit of quickly responding to an infant's needs, the other is likely to accommodate that habit by failing to respond. This pattern then calcifies over days and weeks and months and years."[94] As this pattern continues, competency in one parent increases and competency in the other stagnates, resulting in one parent becoming better equipped at childcare through the ongoing opportunity for practice. When the primary caretaking defaults to the mother, the father is in the secondary care-taking role. "In a number of ways, assuming the secondary role stacks the deck against equality from day one—not due to so-called hardwiring but because of the failure to wire in the absence of experience. That is, the failure to learn."[95] Complementarian claims about women being given "special gifts" that men do not share, and pseudo-scientific claims about biological differences between gender do not hold up.[96] However, cultural conditioning paired with everyday practice has successfully and effectively separated genders into differing parenting roles.

COMPLEMENTARIANISM AND INTENSIVE MOTHERING

Furthering the complementarian agenda, the complementarian approach to motherhood comes with its own celebrity moms, in the form of pastors' wives, especially the megachurch variety. These women "must be hardworking but not competitive, polished but not fussy, wholesome but not perfect. And as famous women, they must do what all famous women do and pretend to be average, subject to the acid test of 'relatability.'"[97] These

---

93. Lockman, *All the Rage*, ch. 2.
94. Lockman, *All the Rage*, ch. 2.
95. Lockman, *All the Rage*, ch. 2.
96. Biology does prepare both women and men for childcare, at least at some level, as the discussion on hormonal changes during and after pregnancy demonstrates. It would be inaccurate from a faith perspective to claim that God has not gifted women to care for children. However, this gifting is not exclusive to women but is gifted to all who would be parents.
97. Bowler, *Preacher's Wife*, intro.

women were living examples of the pushback of the Religious Right against the Women's Movement, giving credibility to the complementarian platform; they can teach complementarian ideals without coming across as dominating and self-serving, as their husbands would.[98] With their large platforms, celebrity pastors' wives are portrayed as the epitome of Christian womanhood, "religious reflections of almost-mythic American ideals of women as wives and mothers, pillars and martyrs, in a culture divided over whether women should lean in or opt out."[99] Along with the move of secular celebrity moms to online platforms, "in the 2000s, a new cast of celebrity 'mommy bloggers' wrote about finding God in laundry, friendship, and ordinary suburbia."[100] Finally, this genre's "newest stars were Home and Garden Television Network reality show rehabbers like Joanna Gaines and Jen Hatmaker (women literally building Christian homes), or Shauna Niequist, daughter of Bill Hybels, whose latest bestseller asked women to be *Present Over Perfect*, eschewing the stress of work for more time at home."[101]

Secular and complementarian philosophies on motherhood intertwine with and reinforce each other, adding to the burdens placed on real-life, individual mothers. The perspective that views of contemporary (secular) motherhood mirror, and even support, complementarianism may seem surprising at first. However, it becomes less so when you consider the historical evidence of patriarchy within the church. In her book *The Making of Biblical Womanhood*, Beth Alison Barr explains, "Patriarchy exists in the Bible because the Bible was written in a patriarchal world. Historically speaking, there is nothing surprising about biblical stories and passages riddled with patriarchal attitudes and actions. What is surprising is how many biblical passages and stories undermine, rather than support, patriarchy."[102] However, "instead of looking different in how we treated women, Christians looked just like everyone else."[103] This confirms that "Patriarchy is created by people, not ordained by God."[104]

98. Bowler, *Preacher's Wife*, ch. 2.

99. Bowler, *Preacher's Wife*, intro. To a lesser extent, many women in the role of "pastor's wife" experience these same pressures stemming from their local congregations. While this phenomenon appears mainly invisible to the male-dominated, Christian academic world, the anecdotal evidence to support this claim is abundant.

100. Bowler, *Preacher's Wife*, ch. 2.

101. Bowler, *Preacher's Wife*, ch. 2.

102. Barr, *Making of Biblical Womanhood*, 36.

103. Barr, *Making of Biblical Womanhood*, 28.

104. Barr, *Making of Biblical Womanhood*, 29. It is important to note that accepted

Mothers Today

The church has often mirrored and bolstered secular expectations of womanhood, including motherhood, rather than redefine them. This viewpoint, with its insistence on female submission to "male headship," echoes colonial-era parenting in many ways. This viewpoint has also added to the cacophony of today's motherhood expectations. Mothers now must be vigilant, moral, self-sacrificing, child-centered, and experts in science and psychology. Mothers must be on guard against abduction or abuse. Mothers must replicate the life of celebrity moms and mommy influencers (including Christian mommy influencers), carrying the bulk of the responsibilities of the home and possibly a career (although this career must never appear important in comparison to their children or threaten the headship of men). Mothers must serve as submissive helpers, shouldering the responsibility of home and childcare in their preordained, feminine role. Mothers do this not only because of societal expectations but also because of religious ones: they believe this is what God expects. Given this historical layering of expectations, is it any wonder that the real-life women discussed at the beginning of this book felt overwhelmed with their mothering roles?

The belief that it is a mother's primary, God-ordained role to mother in this specific way, prohibits many women from questioning this patriarchal system of motherhood. One author shares her experience studying the complementarian manifesto, *Recovering Biblical Manhood and Womanhood*: "Some parts of the book were difficult for me to swallow. And yet its teaching was sown throughout the trusted radio programs, books, and corners of the Internet where the 'good' conservative Christians gleaned. And that's what I wanted to be: good and conservative."[105] Another shares, "We believed that biblical womanhood was biblical. . . . It had become a gospel issue—intertwined with the very nature of God. It had become God's timeless truth, defended by those who remain the most faithful."[106] She further explains, "I had fallen for the biggest lie of all: that adhering to complementarianism is the only option for those who believe the Bible is the authoritative Word of God."[107] These women are not the only ones to fall for the lie that being a Christian equals being a complementarian.

---

patriarchy is one of many cultural responses. "A number of female theologians at elite universities responded warmly to the call for raised consciousness" from the Women's Movement "and, in doing so, opened up a new academic field: feminist theology." Bowler, *Preacher's Wife*, ch. 2. Feminist theology remains a thriving field today.

105. Byrd, *Recovering from Biblical Manhood*, ch. 4.
106. Barr, *Making of Biblical Womanhood*, 199.
107. Barr, *Making of Biblical Womanhood*, 204.

Further, even those mothers who do not adhere to complementarian ideals may still be inclined to adhere to intensive mothering ideals, conflating these with their Christian faith.

The high expectations placed on mothers today, now "sanctified" and heightened by religious institutions, leave women who desire to be both good mothers and good Christians little choice. Even though they are set up to fail (Who could achieve these unrealistically high standards?), they must invest entirely in motherhood, regardless of the cost to themselves or society. Make no mistake, there is a cost. Society is deprived of countless potential contributions that may have otherwise been generated by women whose focus cannot humanly extend beyond their homes and children. As discussed above, women have sacrificed their careers, their free time, and their physical and emotional health for the cause of intensive mothering. They have also unknowingly sacrificed their spiritual health. Miller-McLemore writes of the "critical temptation" women face as they participate in the "religious sensibilities of a divine nature" and become mothers. Understanding and responding with love to a child as described above "demands abandoning one's own point of view, or at least moving the self slightly off-center to meet acute needs. Hence the different temptation for many women, particularly mothers: the temptation to lose oneself."[108] This temptation appears especially acute when considering the cultural contexts of complementarianism and intensive mothering women face. Many women today increasingly find their primary identities as mothers rather than as Christians. They lose their authentic selves as persons created fully in the image of God. They are even misled to believe that to be Christian, as mothers, they must be *this kind* of mother. This belief leads to stressed lives and the state of feeling constantly overwhelmed, along with a loss of identity in Christ. Diane Leclerc puts this misplaced identity in clear terms, referring to this practice as "relational idolatry," reminding readers that children can become idols to their parents when children are prioritized over God.[109] With this understanding, "No longer is the home the means of personal piety; it has now become a potential spiritual hindrance."[110] This is a high cost indeed.

---

108. Miller-McLemore, *Also a Mother*, 92.

109. For a complete discussion on relational idolatry from a Wesleyan Holiness perspective, see Leclerc, *Singleness of Heart*.

110. Leclerc, *Singleness of Heart*, 122.

Mothers Today

How can mothers make sense of the many messages insistent on dictating how they live? American culture, including American church culture, implies that a "true woman" is a mother first, sacrificing all for her children and family. Is this what the Bible implies? What examples of mothers and mothering are found in Scripture? How has the Christian church interpreted this throughout history, and who has the church held up as examples of Christian womanhood? What are the traditions of the Christian faith community? What is the role of these examples in equipping today's mothers to filter through the cacophony of voices, discerning approaches to mothering and identity? How does a Christian mother determine which voices to listen to, which to dismiss, and ultimately, where her identity lies? How do we find God in the midst of mothering? This project hopes to deconstruct the contemporary "cult of true womanhood" as previously outlined and defined as intensive and complementarian mothering. This deconstruction of intensive and complementarian mothering will be accomplished through examining examples and expectations of mothers depicted in Scripture and church history. This book then aims to issue a call to the evangelical church to disciple mothers to form their primary identities as followers of Christ, rather than as mothers.

2

Mothers in Christian Scripture

JESSICA HELD THE INVITATION in her hand and sighed. Another mother–daughter event at church. Another opportunity to learn more about how she had failed as a wife and mother. Hadn't she already learned this enough? She had long known she was suspect at events like this, with her beautiful but mismatched children, her oldest bearing the dark complexion of her first husband and her younger children the fair skin of her second husband, now her second ex. While she was proud of her children, the evidence was impossible to hide. She had a checkered history, which meant she didn't fit in. And now, another event that would highlight for her all the ways she had yet to measure up.

She had tried; hadn't she tried? When her first husband disappeared overnight, before their baby was even born, hadn't she waited for him, hoping with her entire being for his return? Then, when he returned for a peek at their newborn, hadn't her heart broken as he left for good, this time with another woman? That relationship had been passionate and short-lived, but she would have returned to it instantly, even after all these years.

This was not the case with her second husband. If her first husband had broken her heart, her second had broken her spirit. Jessica reviewed the highlights—children she loved, a home she loved, and a husband she couldn't trust. Still, when he wanted to move away from all she knew and loved, away from any sense of home or support, she had dutifully followed his lead. Wasn't this what the church expected, what the Bible taught? That she respect her husband's leadership and act as the submissive wife for the good of her family? Wasn't this her most important calling? She ended up in a house they couldn't afford, with an unreliable husband who was always gone and children struggling in their new environments. Even still, they managed to adjust. Jessica found a church, and her husband signed off on their attending. Her children found new friends and new rhythms. Eventually, she even found a part-time job at their church. This job was a lifeline for her; she felt she was good at it and she enjoyed the work. She felt trapped at home and this was her escape.

What failed to adjust was her marriage. It had been rocky before, but this move seemed to embolden her husband; their money issues, which had always been a problem, worsened. Before, when they would disagree on purchases, she had been able to keep a hold on their family finances. How would she do that if she followed her husband's lead? As she thought the Bible instructed, she needed to let that go if she wanted to live as a good Christian wife and mother. When she did, hoping her husband would step up and act responsibly, he instead went crazy with their money. It seemed he made frivolous purchases solely to prove to her that he could—then *she* had to follow up with a call to *her* parents to ask for money to cover the bills. This had been their pattern for years now; somehow, she was the one to carry the responsibility and shame for his poor decisions.

Jessica had been excited when she landed that part-time job, thinking it would help ease their financial struggles. However, as soon as her paycheck hit their joint bank account, it was gone, claimed by the "burden of leadership" exercised by her husband, now her ex. Even still, hadn't she prioritized her family, putting their needs ahead of hers? She had to scrounge to do it, but she managed to put food on the table and produce thrifted clothing for their children. It took every last ounce of energy, but she did it. Isn't that what a mother does for her children?

The death toll of their marriage came when her husband finally came clean to their pastor about their relationship struggles. Although Jessica had sought pastoral counsel for their relationship many times, she had only been encouraged to emulate the women of the Bible and act as the submissive wife, following her husband's lead. After all, he was the head of the household and was better positioned to know what was needed. Any pushback to this strategy or questions beyond this philosophy fell on deaf ears.

However, her job suddenly ended when her husband went to the pastor. Her lifeline in an otherwise depressing life was gone. No matter that her husband was dishonest, impoverished their family, or was rarely home. She never knew if she could believe him, but she knew she couldn't depend on him. No matter that these were the issues they had faced since the beginning of their relationship, before their children, before their move, and before her job. The reason for their relationship troubles had been diagnosed—Jessica didn't spend enough time at home because of her part-time job at the church. Now, there was no job, so she could go home and emulate those women of the Bible, becoming the perfect wife and mother, just like they were. The women of the Bible may have been able to do it, but Jessica could not. She tried, but the increased depression that followed her job loss soon led to her second divorce—yet another mark against her.

Looking at the women's event invitation, Jessica reasoned that although she no longer needed to worry about being the perfect wife, she still needed work on becoming that "perfect Christian mother." She admitted that after all that time, all that effort, and all that loss, she still wasn't living up to those standards. She was still not measuring up to what was most important. She agreed that whatever sacrifice she made on her children's behalf was worth it, and she marked the event down on her calendar.

How do the expectations placed on today's mother line up with the Christian faith? There is a full spectrum of teachings available to Christian mothers, ranging from practical "how-to" tips, to how to fit into the idealized family structure (which often includes the "equal but subordinate" position for mothers discussed in the previous chapter), to how to apply biblical principles to the pressures of daily motherhood. Even still, mothers in the church often attempt to model their lives of faith and lives as mothers after male examples and complementarian or intensive mothering ideals. Do the teachings of today's more conservative churches on motherhood, including these ideals, line up with what the Bible says about mothers living in faith? Of note, Christian woman need not be in an evangelical context that embraces complementarianism. Even Christian mothers whose families and churches embrace what they believe to be biblical—the egalitarian model—still stress over-perfectionism in their mothering. It is quite important to ask, How did women living in biblical eras approach life, mothering, and God? What did they learn and experience? How can today's mothering experience be informed by their history? As Christianity is built on the content of the Bible, what examples of mothers and mothering are found in Scripture for Christian mothers today? This chapter will explore the contexts of the Old and New Testaments as they pertain to mothers; the life stories of the biblical mothers Eve, Sarah, Hagar, Rebekah, Leah, Rachel, Bilhah, Zilpah, Hannah, and Mary; implications for today's mother will be offered as well. What matters most in the life of a Christian mother?

OLD TESTAMENT CONTEXT

To understand the lives of biblical mothers more fully, it is important to have a basic understanding of the culture in which they lived. Reading the Old Testament can leave the impression of a large, semi-developed country with a robust governance structure in place, in addition to a large metropolis capital city, Jerusalem, during the Iron Age, the time period of the early Old Testament. Yet in actuality, while "The 'Land of Israel' may loom large in our imagination because of its biblical role . . . it occupies a very small part of the larger Fertile Crescent . . . no more than about 90 by 150 miles."[1] Further, while modern readers may picture bustling city life, the Hebrew word for city "often designates settlement types that were not really cities," instead, "they were tiny villages or hamlets, most with several dozen dwellings, housing fewer than several hundred people. And they are all agricultural settlements, as was the case for most settlements throughout the Iron Age."[2] It is not until later, during the Iron Age II period that populations increased, the monarchy was established, and larger settlements with fortified walls developed, although these were still relatively small.[3]

This background significantly affected the lives of all who lived in that region during that period, including mothers. Their efforts were needed alongside their families' to ensure the survival of all. In the agrarian context of subsistence farming, women's work (including mother's work) was necessary to the family economy and therefore valued. Research into the culture of the early Old Testament does not reveal a society so patriarchal that it is misogynistic. Instead, life for mothers and other women during this time period occurred within a community in the truest sense of the word. Life was difficult for those who were mothers, yes, but that was because life was difficult for everyone, not because mothers were specifically female rather than male. In addition, everyone's contributions were valued because

---

1. Meyers, *Rediscovering Eve*, 39.

2. Meyers, *Rediscovering Eve*, 40–41.

3. Meyers, *Rediscovering Eve*, 41. This development during the Iron Age II period also encompasses the time period of the Old Testament, which spans thousands of years.

life was extremely difficult. Women's daily work was as necessary as men's for survival, and fathers contributed to family life just as mothers did. "The traditional concept of men as breadwinners and women as homemakers must be set aside; otherwise, the role and meaning of women's economic and other roles in ancient Israel will be obscured."[4] While women, and women who were mothers, did not have many vocational options, this was not because they were systemically discriminated against, but rather because that was how life was for everyone. In addition, mothers in this community benefited from working alongside others who shared the same purpose: survival.[5]

Author Carol Meyers uses "Everywoman Eve" as an archetype for women living in the Old Testament context; this woman would have lived her life in an agrarian context. Her days would have been filled with the extensive tasks required for food production, including grinding, bread baking and building the equipment necessary for this production, such as grindstones and ovens, often crafted in cooperation with other women of the community. She would have lived with her family unit, including her husband's parents, and in a settlement with extended family. She would have taken the lead in many religious practices in the home as these practices overlapped with celebrations and healthcare. As the family member who connected with other family units regularly (for example, while communally grinding and baking daily bread, preparing food for a celebration, or assisting with healthcare) and who herself originated in a different family before joining and living with her husband's family, she would have maintained essential social connections for the group.

Childcare would have been a regular part of daily life. As a mother, "Everywoman Eve" would take primary responsibility for her young children. This responsibility would be shared with the other women of the home, and family structures prescribed that there were usually other women in the home. As soon as sons were old enough to be helpful, responsibility for training them passed from mothers to fathers as sons accompanied their fathers to the fields where they were trained in skills necessary to their way of life. Daughters would remain at home with their mothers and grandmothers, assisting with the daily workload. Parenting would not have been

---

4. Meyers, *Rediscovering Eve*, 121.
5. Meyers, *Rediscovering Eve*, 38–52.

considered a separate vocation in itself as it often is today, but rather an integrated part of everyday life.[6]

It is also helpful to keep in mind that while in today's context, the Bible in its entirety, including its history, law, and moral codes, is readily available, that was not the case for "Everywoman Eve" and her contemporaries, including the matriarchs and other biblical women discussed below. In fact,

> There was no Hebrew Bible at all, at least not as a canonical whole, until centuries after the Iron Age, long after Israelite culture had morphed into its successor, early Judaism. Moreover, it was not until late in the history of ancient Israel that some of the materials comprising the Hebrew Bible were collected and deemed authoritative. To be sure, many tales, aphorisms, and other genres would have circulated orally before then and may have been widely known. Yet, for most of the hundreds of years of Israelite existence in the Iron Age not only was the Bible not accessible, but actually there was no such thing as the Bible in anything close to the form we now take for granted.[7]

Even once these early materials began to be formalized and carry religious authority, it may have had little relevance to the life of the average mother. "Much of the Hebrew Bible was produced by the literary activity of a small, unrepresentative segment of the Israelite population: literate elite men in an urban context. Biblical information about nonurban women comes from sources hierarchically and demographically removed from them."[8] This is important to note when examining these early histories; care must be taken not to read assumptions into the text about biblical knowledge on the part of the characters. For example, laws against incest and instructions prohibiting multiple wives eventually became part of the biblical canon, but the women referenced here predate these instructions.[9] We also need to acknowledge that when we hear a woman's voice in Scripture, it is a woman's voice that was interpreted through and recorded by a man.[10]

---

6. For a full discussion on this topic, see Meyers, *Rediscovering Eve*, 38–58.
7. Meyers, *Rediscovering Eve*, 19.
8. Meyers, *Rediscovering Eve*, 22.
9. For example, 1 Tim 3:2 and Lev 18; 20.
10. This is one of many examples that demonstrates how the distinction between "divine inspiration" of Scripture and "mechanical dictation" of Scripture makes a significant impact on interpretation.

EVE

There are many traditions and interpretations of the first woman and mother. Eve's story has been occasionally used to uplift women, but generally to excuse millennia of male oppression. "Consequently, we inevitably look at it through [history's] interpretive eyes without realizing that translations and expositions of Genesis 1–3 may distort or misrepresent the meaning and function of the tale in its Israelite context."[11] In addition to understanding the cultural background above, there are several points in the Eve narrative that need to be clarified, as it has inappropriately been used to subjugate women throughout history. An overview for context is helpful, since mothers throughout history have been treated per interpretations of Eve, even unconsciously. For one, the translation that Eve was explicitly created to be a "helper" to Adam has lent itself to the idea that Eve is to be subordinate to Adam. This issue was addressed in chapter 1, concluding that Eve instead was created to live and work with Adam as an equal partner. In addition to the "helper" discussion, it is sometimes assumed that Eve is to be subordinate to Adam because she was created second, designating Adam as the leader solely because he was created first. In contrast, Cowles reminds readers when speaking of 1 Corinthians,

> It is of vital importance, however, to note that *Paul challenges and destroys the traditionalist "order of creation" rationale*. . . . "Nevertheless, in the Lord woman is not independent of man or man independent of woman. *For just as woman came from man, so man comes through woman*; but all things come from God" (11:11–12). True, the first woman originated from the man. Lest prideful man be tempted to lord it over the woman—as indeed has been the case—God ordained that after the first Adam, every man would originate from a woman.[12]

If order corresponds with value, the plants and animals should be seen as the most valuable, since God created them first; or, if we reverse the order and see gradations of value going upward, "man" was not created last, "woman" was. This, of course, is the creation narrative of Gen 1. Genesis 2 gives a different account, and most scholars believe that this may be the joining of multiple writers, writing at different times. In Gen 2, humanity is created first, as "no shrub had yet appeared on the earth" (2:5).

---

11. Meyers, *Rediscovering Eve*, 60.
12. Cowles, *Woman's Place?*, 112 (emphasis added).

According to the second chapter of Genesis, the original human was formed by God from "the dust of the ground" (Gen 2:7). This "signifies humanity as cultivators of the arable land outside of Eden: agrarians were to be of the same material essence as the soil of their fields."[13] Eve is often assumed to be inferior to Adam because she was created through more than dust, needing a part of Adam's physical body to come into being, as described in Gen 2:21–22. However, "The *tzelaʿ* that 'God removes is a 'side' and not a 'rib' as commonly mistranslated."[14] It is possible, then, to understand Eve as a completion of Adam and that both came from dust, or, even more intriguing, that Adam refers to an androgynous being who only became gendered when Eve is created. According to one scholar, "They are two halves of a whole. They are neither identical nor mirror images. Together and individually they reflect the divine image."[15] While the partners making up the beginning of humanity (Eve and Adam) were still one person, according to this theory, God "formed every animal of the field and every bird of the air, and brought them to the [person]" for them to be named. The combined human "gave names to all cattle, and to the birds of the air, and to every animal of the field" (Gen 2:19–20). That this act of naming animals occurred while Eve and Adam are combined as one person is significant, as "naming was a way in which a power relationship is established. Adam is given authority over the creation, and his dominion is demonstrated through the act of naming."[16] Combined, the first human demonstrates dominion over the rest of creation through giving names. Following this theory, however, the naming of Eve as "Woman" is not an act of dominion, but the act of separation, whereby we truly now have an Adam who is gendered, and an Eve who is gendered. Yet they remain interdependent as two types of human; they are both equally created in the divine image, both male and female.

If, as we assert, Eve and Adam were "two halves of the same whole," Eve was not only equal with Adam, but she was also present with him, beginning when God first formed them, combined together, from the dust of the earth. This understanding removes the argument that Eve was less responsible for obeying God's command not to eat fruit from the tree of the knowledge of good and evil, as if she received this command secondhand

---

13. Meyers, *Rediscovering Eve*, 71.
14. Gafney, *Womanist Midrash*, 21.
15. Gafney, *Womanist Midrash*, 22.
16. Bronner, *Stories of Biblical Mothers*, 2.

through Adam. Eve was responsible for herself, as was Adam. According to Meyers, God "instructs the person about what can and cannot be eaten . . . with both female and male contained in this androgynous being, both are recipients of God's directives."[17] Eve was equal with Adam and she was equally responsible for her decision to eat this particular fruit; as part of the original human, she received this command firsthand from God, just as Adam did. But just as important is the understanding that Eve is not *more* responsible than Adam, which has created a type of original misogyny that has carried throughout Christian history![18]

The story of the Fall is full of complexities reflected in the human situation. Eve, in conversation with the crafty serpent, discovers that there are other possible paths forward, and thus "awakes" out of what Paul Tillich calls a "dreaming innocence."[19] Eve had been instructed by God against eating the fruit and was fully aware of this instruction. However, she also recognized "that the tree was good for food, and that it was a delight to the eyes, and the tree was to be desired to make one wise, she took of its fruit and ate" (Gen 3:6). According to Lapsley, "This action is recounted rapidly and without fuss, gesturing to its inherent inevitability—human beings, both women and men, are characterized by their ability to discern good from bad."[20] Lapsley seems to be leaning into the more Neo-Orthodox theory (*à la* Reinhold Niebuhr) that the fall was, in fact, in some sense inevitable. But Niebuhr insists that it was *not necessary*; it was not predetermined in any way, lest God become the author of sin.[21]

This moment has been widely interpreted as the first sin of humanity (the Bible itself does not attach the term "sin" to this occurrence). Following Lapsley's assumptions, she finally pronounces that "the woman chooses adulthood, a full, complex moral anthropology. The woman's reaching up

---

17. Meyers, *Rediscovering Eve*, 73.

18. In the quest to demonstrate that Eve was equal to Adam and therefore women are equal to men, it is essential to remember the whole picture. While Eve has traditionally and unfairly borne the brunt of the blame for the biblical fall and its subsequent hardships, and the rest of *woman*kind with her, when adjusting views of this narrative to accurately reflect the Genesis account, it is not appropriate to shift blame entirely to Adam and *man*kind. This blame-shifting is also unfair and fails to reflect Genesis accurately. As equally created in the image of God, the original creation pair, along with all humanity after them, share equal responsibility.

19. Tillich, *Existence and the Christ*, 33.

20. Lapsley, *Whispering the Word*, 17.

21. Niebuhr, *Human Nature*, 242.

into the tree to grasp the enticing fruit inaugurates a new era for humanity, characterized by true choice and the privilege and responsibility of interpreting their world."[22] She is even brazen enough to say that Eve has chosen wisdom, the knowledge of good and evil and the responsibility that comes with that knowledge. Others have suggested that the serpent's temptation by uttering the words "you will be like God" could be seen as Eve misinterpreting of her sense of being created in the image of God and its implicit call to be God-like (as in holy). This is certainly an even further step to seeing Eve's decision sympathetically. But while Lapsley suggests that Eve is choosing maturity and wisdom through eating the fruit, Meyers (who also seems sympathetic to Eve) makes clear that "in eating the appealing fruit the first couple makes a decidedly unwise move. They disobey God. The consequence is not only mortality but also the reality of agrarian life anticipated at the beginning of the Eden episode and prescribed in its closing section."[23]

This portion of the narrative revolves around Eve; however, the decision to eat the fruit was not made by Eve alone. Instead, this was a choice made by the couple. Eve has often been characterized as tempting or even seducing Adam to convince him to eat the "forbidden fruit." The word forbidden has often been sexualized. But, as Barbara MacHaffie points out, "Nowhere in the story is the woman accused of seducing the male. Rather, the verb 'to seduce' or 'to deceive' is used only in connection with the serpent's activities. Nowhere does the story say that the woman tempted the man or used wicked persuasion."[24] Adam made a fully informed decision, equally capable of choosing for himself. If anything, he is overly dependent here on Eve's influence, not because of some fault in Eve but perhaps because of a weakness in Adam.[25] Although we are not apprised of his motivation as we are with Eve, Adam was present for the conversation with the serpent. Adam also was able to discern that the fruit was good for food, pleasing to the eye, and a potential source of wisdom. Adam, too, made the complex decision to eat the fruit. This understanding removes Eve's culpability for

---

22. Lapsley, *Whispering the Word*, 17.
23. Meyers, *Rediscovering Eve*, 80.
24. MacHaffie, *Her Story*, 13.
25. It is important here to avoid the implication that Adam should seek to compensate for this possible dependence or weakness, found within himself, by attempting to control another person, Eve. A more appropriate implication would be that Adam needs to take responsibility for and control *his* behavior, just as Eve needs to do for *her* behavior. The same is true for the interactions of men and women today.

Adam's actions; just as Eve was, Adam was responsible for himself and the consequences of his own decision.

This decision, made by both Eve and Adam, does, in fact, lead to the knowledge of good and evil, as "the eyes of both were opened" (Gen 3:7). It also leads to both hiding from God and an eventual conversation with God.

> As the story unfolds, the biblical authors focus on Adam and subordinate Eve. God does not. God kills for Eve, sews for Eve, clothes Eve. God made tunics for Eve and her man from skins. . . . God had said that on the day that the humans ate from the forbidden tree, on that day they would surely die. Instead, unidentified animals die. Then . . . Eve and Adam are banished together . . . the whole of humanity, even when there are only two of them.[26]

God champions both, not only Adam, in the aftermath of their disobedient decision. The lives of both Eve and Adam change drastically at this point and all of history follows. "Genesis 3:17–19 mandates exhausting labor for men, and 5:16 orders women to work hard and have multiple pregnancies. Together these passages reflect the Israelite environmental and demographic context. They explain and validate the hardships of agrarian life in Iron Age Israel."[27]

Eve (and therefore womanhood in general) is often put in subjugation to men as a result of the curse recorded in Gen 3:14–19 and specifically as it relates to Eve in Gen 3:16. This is misleading, however, as only the serpent and the ground are cursed in this passage; the verse addressing Eve can be more accurately translated as, "I will make great your toil and many your pregnancies; with hardship shall you have children. Your turning is to your man/husband, and he shall rule/control you [sexually]."[28] Although physical pain is not excluded, "hardship" here refers mainly to the "mental anguish" of motherhood, which parents of every generation can relate to, whether or not they had access to painkillers. Further, in a context where maternal and infant mortality rates were extremely high, and the childbirth experience traumatized those giving birth, a directive is included in this verse to ensure the continuation of humanity in "he shall rule/control you [sexually]."[29] "Neither the ancient function nor the interpretive development is attractive to most contemporary readers. But having the ideology

---

26. Gafney, *Womanist Midrash*, 26.
27. Meyers, *Rediscovering Eve*, 101.
28. Meyers, *Rediscovering Eve*, 102.
29. Meyers, *Rediscovering Eve*, 102.

of the text placed in a historically contingent context, in which it would have benefited the household and community, contests the validity of the interpretive ideology and highlights its positive function."[30]

Eve becomes the first mother in this historical and theological setting. "Eve's language is remarkable; she speaks of having 'created,' implying pleasure, rather than having 'birthed,' suggesting pain. Her role as new mother emphasizes her joy. . . . She conveys gladness, stressing the personal pronoun 'I,' and boasting in her creative power."[31] Eve, in partnership with God, birthed the first child, symbolically becoming the mother of all the living. In one sense, Eve becomes the first cocreator with God. Eve named her sons Cain and Abel, and through this naming process, "Eve rejoices in her generative powers and shows that motherhood is a privilege rather than a punishment."[32] However, "there is subtle irony here: the mother of all living has given birth to the father of murder (Cain), who is inscribed in Scripture as the first to succumb to sin on earth,"[33] since the fall is not labeled as sin in previous chapters. In addition to labor and childbirth, this was also a consequence of Eve's decision to pursue knowledge of good and evil; now she knew both. "When she has another son, she names him Seth, meaning 'God has provided me with another offspring in place of Abel,' for Cain had killed him (Genesis 4:25). Here Eve realizes that there are limitations to her power as Mother of Life, and gives thanks to God for replacing her dead son with Seth."[34] Eve, the archetypal mother, is the first to birth a child and the first mother to mourn a child.

Is Eve a fitting biblical example for today's mother? Eve, fully created in the image of God and an equal helper to her partner Adam, was initially formed from the dust of the earth as a combined human, with Adam. As a combined human, they established dominion over the rest of creation by naming animals. Eve was then taken from the combined human's dust-created side and formed into her own person. Rather than a tempting seductress acting on secondhand instruction, Eve makes an informed decision, choosing wisdom and the knowledge of good and evil, along with all that comes with that knowledge; Adam makes the same decision. As Eve lives through the resulting events of this decision, she is championed by

---

30. Meyers, *Rediscovering Eve*, 102.
31. Bronner, *Stories of Biblical Mothers*, 3.
32. Bronner, *Stories of Biblical Mothers*, 3.
33. Gafney, *Womanist Midrash*, 27.
34. Bronner, *Stories of Biblical Mothers*, 3.

God even as her "adult" choice leads to "adult" consequences. These consequences include hard work and the need to procreate to save humanity from extinction, because she is now finite (as traditionally understood). This intricate sequence of events leads to Eve becoming the first mother. As a mother, she experiences hardship, joy, heartbreak, and comfort; she knows and experiences both good and evil. She is known as the mother of all the living, the mother of all other mothers; yet her narrative overflows the boundaries of patriarchal motherhood. As this complex, sophisticated example stands in contrast to today's ideal of intensive, complementarian motherhood, it has the potential to resonate with the complex lives of real women who are mothers today.

SARAH AND HAGAR

This background of the Eve/Mother archetype sets the stage for the historical figures of the Matriarchs of Israel, beginning with Sarah. Sarah begins her story as Sarai; she is the younger half sister and wife of Abraham (also Abram). This is an incestuous mix of relationships Abraham takes advantage of to his own benefit. When he feared for his own life because neighboring kings noticed Sarah's beauty, Abraham did not hesitate to capitalize on the "sister" portion of their relationship but conceal the "wife" aspect, giving her away to be part of another man's harem. This action results in sparing Abraham from violence (although the same cannot be said for Sarah). This action also enriches him as he was subsequently the recipient of gifts in exchange for his sister-wife. This series of events occurs twice in the biblical text (Gen 12 and 20), although in the second occurrence it is made clear that the king does not go near Sarah. Sarah appears as a strong character with her own agency in later narratives, however these accounts make clear that there were limits on this agency, subject to her brother-husband's approval. If it were not for God's intervention, Sarah's story in the history of Israel would have ended there as the concubine of either Pharaoh or King Abimelech. Thankfully, "God restores some measure of personhood to Sarai. To God, she is not just any woman: she is Sarai, Abram's wife, and God has plans for her. So God intervenes."[35] The poor treatment she receives from the men in these passages deepens the complexity of her later treatment of her servant Hagar.

---

35. Frymer-Kensky, *Reading the Women*, 95.

Although Sarah eventually became a matriarch, she lived until her senior years before birthing a child. "She endured a long period of shameful barrenness with some forbearance. . . . Although Sarah had lived assertively for the bulk of her life as a dominant and barren matriarch, she most strongly emerges as a distinct voice in the biblical text during situations relating to her fertility and subsequent motherhood."[36] It is clear Sarah is passionate about both becoming a mother and protecting her child, going to exaggerated and questionable lengths to accomplish both. Sarah eventually gave birth to a son, Isaac, but not until after she had complicated family relationships by inserting her servant Hagar into the mix.

Hagar is not listed among the matriarchs; as she is an Egyptian rather than an Israelite and becomes the mother of "other" nations, she is not a matriarch of Israel. However, she is an early example of motherhood in the Bible. Interestingly, it could be argued that she followed God to a greater degree than most other biblical characters: mothers, fathers, women, and men included.

> Hagar's story provides an interesting foil to the stories of the matriarchs. Though she is a mere servant, she . . . experiences multiple theophanies. Unlike many of the other women of Genesis she does not struggle with barrenness or experience any trouble in conceiving. However, her encounter with motherhood, though seemingly welcome, almost instantly brings turmoil and strife.[37]

Hagar enters the scene at Sarah's behest. In her barren old age, Sarah concludes that she will not be able to birth children for Abraham, but perhaps she could provide a child for him through her servant Hagar. Sarah was twice given by Abraham to others, once preceding this incident with Hagar and once after. Nonetheless, Sarah gives Hagar to Abraham for the specific purpose of bearing a child. Sarah's intent was to claim any resulting child as her own. When Hagar does indeed conceive, conflict arises between the two women, and Sarah, after complaining about the situation to Abraham and getting his permission, treats Hagar "harshly" (Gen 16:6). "The Bible is clear of the traumatic triangle involving Abraham-Hagar-Sarah. Hagar's position as slave, Sarah's barrenness, and Abraham's patriarchal acquiescence make for a perfect storm."[38] Further, "The biblical text makes

---

36. Bronner, *Stories of Biblical Mothers*, 9.
37. Bronner, *Stories of Biblical Mothers*, 9.
38. Buckhanon Crowder, *When Momma Speaks*, ch. 4.

plain the unwelcome truth that women participate in the trafficking and sexual abuse of other women. Understandably, Hagar runs away."[39]

After running away, Hagar encounters the angel of the Lord in the wilderness. Although she is instructed to return to her oppressors and submit to them, she also "receives the first divine annunciation to a woman in the canon of a promised child and promise of a dynasty. Hagar will become the Mother of Many Peoples."[40] In addition, this "portion of Hagar's story contains an episode without peer in all of Scripture. In Genesis 16:13, Hagar names God: *El Ro'i*, 'God of seeing,' . . . she is the only person in the canon to give God a name."[41] Hagar returns and births her son Ishmael; although Sarah's original intent was to claim Hagar's child as her own, she does not do so.

Sarah was indeed responsible for providing Abraham with a son through Hagar, a circumstance that would not have occurred without her direction. However, God did not intend to establish a covenant with Abraham's son, Ishmael, as God made clear in Gen 16:18–19. Although God did bless Ishmael and cause him to father nations, Sarah is to bear a son herself, which she did well past child-bearing age, and this son, Isaac, was to be the recipient of God's covenant. Neither Abraham nor Sarah expected this to happen, as evidenced by their responses of laughter. However, God intervened, and this miracle occurred. It may be assumed that all is now well; Hagar had returned and borne a son who will father nations in his own right, and Sarah had finally become a mother in the true sense of the word rather than the stepmom she seemed briefly to find acceptable. Sarah's son was destined to receive Abraham's inheritance and God's covenant.

While Hagar became a mother by no volition of her own, Sarah had gone to great lengths to become a mother, and once she had, she was fiercely protective of her child. All was not well after all, and "Sarah accosts Abraham to handle Hagar. The current drama is . . . rooted in Sarah's insecurity over her son's future security. Ishmael, born of a slave, will not share the inheritance of her son."[42] This resulted in Hagar again sojourning in the wilderness, this time not because she ran away but because she was sent away. Although Sarah wishes to rid herself and her son of any competition, "we should note that in a world in which slavery is accepted, Hagar and

---

39. Gafney, *Womanist Midrash*, 35.
40. Gafney, *Womanist Midrash*, 42.
41. Gafney, *Womanist Midrash*, 43.
42. Buckhanon Crowder, *When Momma Speaks*, ch. 4.

Ishmael are not sold: they are freed. Hagar and Ishmael leave Abraham's household as emancipated slaves."[43]

Although Hagar and Ishmael were now free, they were also desperate. Hagar is the one who seemingly lost out in the conflict between mothers. "As a homeless mother in a nomadic culture, Hagar and her son are at risk for violence and further exploitation. The desert is residence for both human and animal beasts. It is no place for a mother and her teen son."[44] Once the supplies Abraham sent them out with were consumed, they were alone in the wilderness without water, Ishmael was on the verge of death and Hagar could not bear to watch him die. Once again, God intervened. While she wept, "the angel of God called to Hagar from heaven," assured her that Ishmael would become a great nation, and revealed a well of water (Gen 21). The contrast between mothers is striking: "Sarah wanted to be a mother for the sake of cultural honor-shame. The mother in Hagar just wanted her son to live."[45] Due to God's intervention and Hagar's agency, Hagar and Ishmael go on to thrive apart from Sarah and Abraham's provision. "A single mother, she . . . [completes] her parental duties by arranging for [Ishmael's] marriage. Abraham has no role in shaping the future of Hagar and her descendants. . . . God has given Hagar that right by treating her as the head of her own family and lineage."[46] God recognized, validated, and blessed Hagar as the single mom that she was.

One of the most pivotal moments of Sarah's life as a mother occurs without her presence and possibly without her knowledge. Genesis 22 records the account of Abraham taking her son Isaac to one of the mountains in the land of Moriah to offer him as a burnt sacrifice. Abraham would have done exactly that if it were not for God's intervention; Sarah is not mentioned in this passage. This event is apparently between a father, a son, and a saving God. What is interesting is that while it is Abraham who is given credit for being willing to sacrifice his "only son" Isaac, and provides an archetype for the later sacrifice of Jesus, God's only son, Isaac is not Abraham's only son.[47] Instead, Isaac is Sarah's only son. A modern reader may object to this injustice; however,

---

43. Frymer-Kensky, *Reading the Women*, 235.
44. Buckhanon Crowder, *When Momma Speaks*, ch. 4.
45. Buckhanon Crowder, *When Momma Speaks*, ch. 4.
46. Frymer-Kensky, *Reading the Women*, 236.
47. In addition to Ishmael, Abraham later fathered six other sons through his second wife Keturah, after Sarah's death. Genesis 25:2–6 names these sons and their sons.

> according to the social conventions of his time, Abraham . . . had the right to do whatever he would with the members of his family. . . . In Genesis 20, Abraham gives Sarah to Abimelech; in Genesis 21, Abraham sends Ishmael out of his household; in Genesis 22, Abraham is prepared to sacrifice Isaac to God. In all of these stories, the family members and Israel survive because God intervenes to make sure there is no permanent damage to the family. Without this special divine supervision, the rights of the father would have led to disaster for those under his control.[48]

God had a plan for Sarah and Sarah's only son Isaac. These plans did not include barrenness, human trafficking, or human sacrifice.[49]

As with Eve, the stories of Sarah and Hagar overflow the bounds of patriarchal motherhood; neither woman exemplifies intensive, complementarian mothering. Sarah, in an incestuous relationship with her half-brother, was a victim of human trafficking perpetuated by the man who was to be her protector. God's protection and intervention freed her from this situation twice and allowed for her agency. Sarah asserted this agency, which led to a mess of family relationships, including the trafficking of her servant Hagar and making herself a jealous stepmother. Although Sarah complicated the situation, God was still invested and active in Sarah's life; God still championed Sarah, and she birthed a child in her old age.[50] Sarah then faced further complications in her blended family relationships and eventually acted out against Hagar. Later, after fiercely advocating for her only son, she almost lost him anyway, again by the hands of the man who was to be their protector. Hagar found herself entangled in this family drama. She was trafficked, abused, blamed, abandoned, and eventually became a single mother fending for herself and her son. She also experienced the direct working of God in her and her son's life.

This messy blended family containing incest, trafficking, abuse, competition, and a close call regarding child sacrifice, is a far cry from the kind

---

Genesis 25:6 also references other sons birthed through Abraham's concubines. All sons but Isaac were given gifts and sent away.

48. Frymer-Kensky, *Reading the Women*, 97.

49. While this biblical situation between Sarah and Abraham is extreme, contemporary mothers may relate to this account when the fathers of their shared children have custody and parent in ways objectionable to the mothers.

50. Women who delay childbirth and resort to fertility treatments may relate to Sarah's struggle to conceive and to her advanced maternal age. However, Sarah's highly advanced maternal age defies even today's medical achievements and speaks to the miraculous intervention of God.

of family life idealized today. Although this narrative portrays family life far from today's ideal, elements of this biblical family may more accurately portray many contemporary families than the traditional family ideal is capable of portraying. The father of both Sarah and Hagar's children, Abraham is a far cry from the "servant leader husband" prescribed by complementarian ideals or the egalitarian husband envisioned by feminist ideals. While Sarah's passionate mothering may have some overlap with today's mother, she is still a far cry from today's intensive, complementarian motherhood ideals. Hagar, as a single, working, often oppressed mother also fails to meet these standards. Again, her experience may more accurately portray that of many contemporary mothers than traditional ideals can portray.[51] While all of this is accurate, God still redeemed each of them and was intricately involved in their lives; God acted for their good. Any biblical takeaway from this complicated saga does not point to today's unrealistic motherhood ideals. Instead, this takeaway points to the involvement of God working in complicated, messy situations, and complicated, messy lives.

REBEKAH

The power mothers affect within their families is no small thing in any age. This truth is evident in the story of Rebekah. "Rebekah is introduced in Genesis 24 as the key to the fulfillment of God's promise to Abraham."[52] When she first appeared in the biblical text, she arrived as the answer to Eliezar's prayer. This arrival occurred as Eliezar sought a wife for Isaac at his master Abraham's bidding. She immediately revealed active participation in her own story by extending "the offer of hospitality herself (24:25); she does not need to check with anyone. Rebekah's brother Laban does the necessary housework to prepare their mother's house for their guest (see 24:31)."[53] As the story unfolds, this young woman makes her own choice to travel to Isaac and become his wife. "At that moment, it becomes clear that [Rebekah] is the counterpart to both Abraham and Sarah. Like Sarah,

---

51. Another significant contemporary comparison may be found in the experience of the African American mother and by extension, all oppressed mothers. "The story of Hagar became paradigmatic of God's promises to enslaved African mothers. Hagar was a mother who could do nothing but rely on the promise of God to save her and her child. Her story shows that God did indeed save Hagar and her child, suggesting that God would do the same for enslaved women in America." Marga, *In the Image*, 156.

52. Gafney, *Womanist Midrash*, 46.

53. Gafney, *Womanist Midrash*, 47.

she is the instrument of the promise, the agent through whom Isaac will become the father of a nation. She is also a second Abraham, who, like him, voluntarily chooses to leave Mesopotamia for Canaan."[54]

Rebekah was loved by Isaac, which is described in Gen 24. "In verse 67, for the first time in the canon, the relationship between a woman and her man is characterized by love.... Indeed, Isaac's love for Rebekah introduces the verb ... 'love' (including romantic love) into the text."[55] As this is a different verb than the term used to describe God's love, "no previous character in the Scriptures is described as loving or being loved" in this way.[56] This is significant to the discussion on mothers. "We are to understand that in bringing a beloved wife into his mother's tent, Isaac transfers the deep love he had felt for his mother, Sarah, to his spouse, Rebecca."[57] Adding more significance to this occurrence, love and the seeking of love will figure prominently in the narrative of their son and daughters-in-law.

Although Isaac loved Rebekah, he still came dangerously close to the action of trafficking his wife, as did his father Abraham. Genesis 26 explains that when Isaac settled with Rebekah in Gerar, Rebekah's great physical beauty made him afraid to reveal she was his wife, instead claiming she was his sister. This claim was even less true than Abraham's omission, as Rebekah was his cousin rather than his half sister. Isaac let this untruth stand "for a long time" (Gen 26:8), until the king figured out the ruse and confronted Isaac. Ultimately, it was not her loving husband who was her protector, but rather the Philistine king.

Like her mother-in-law/aunt before her, Rebekah was barren. Isaac prayed on her behalf and she became pregnant with twins, but this was not an easy pregnancy. Her sons struggled in her womb to such a degree that although she did not seek God in order to end her barrenness—Isaac did that—she did go directly to God to question this struggle. In response, "God speaks directly to Rebekah, without an intermediary, prophet, or messenger. God promises that both children will become great nations, but they will be divided in an inverted hierarchy, based on their age."[58] This oracle may be the reason behind her later actions in which she acted in favor of her son Jacob at the expense of her son Esau, manipulating family

---

54. Frymer-Kensky, *Reading the Women*, 13.
55. Gafney, *Womanist Midrash*, 48.
56. Gafney, *Womanist Midrash*, 48.
57. Bronner, *Stories of Biblical Mothers*, 8.
58. Gafney, *Womanist Midrash*, 48–49.

interactions to secure the greater birthright and blessing for her favored child.

This "manipulation" occurred in Gen 27, as Isaac prepared to bless his oldest son Esau. Rebekah overheard Isaac's plans and conspired to secure this blessing for Jacob instead. She convinced Jacob to participate in her plan, overcoming his objections and going so far as to promise to take the curse herself if it came to that. "She will take the curse if Jacob will take the risk."[59] Rebekah and Jacob succeeded in procuring Isaac's blessing, intended by Isaac for Esau. This action resulted in understandable discord between the twin brothers. Esau hated Jacob to the extent that Rebekah sent Jacob, running for his life, to the shelter of her brother Laban. In reflecting on this, author Wilda C. Gafney speculates, "Esau's disappointment becomes hatred directed solely toward Jacob (Gen 27:41). I wonder if that means he did not know his mother's role in the loss of his inheritance or if he simply could not bring himself to hate her."[60]

Although today's reader may see in Rebekah's actions a mother inappropriately manipulating the family situation, the patriarchal, iron age context of this narrative reveals Rebekah used the resources she had at her disposal to carry out God's plan. Further, the "biblical world valued cunning in the underdog.... The powerless know that trickery may save their lives. Early interpreters, both Jewish and Christian, praised [Rebekah], as did medieval and reformation writers.... To some contemporary eyes, the

---

59. Gafney, *Womanist Midrash*, 51.

60. Gafney, *Womanist Midrash*, 51. Gafney is significant to this conversation on motherhood and mothering as a womanist theologian and scholar. She clarifies, "Womanism is often simply defined as black feminism.... [But] it is much more.... Womanism shares the radical egalitarianism that characterizes feminism at its basic level, but without its default referent, white women functioning as the exemplar for all women. Feminism here is both the justice work of women on behalf of women in public and private spaces that seeks to transcend boundaries, and feminism as it is in the Western world with historical and contemporary racism, classism, and transphobia characterizing it to differing degrees." Gafney, *Womanist Midrash*, 2–3. "Womanist interpretation does not privilege the embodiment and experiences of black women at the expense of other members of the interpretive community.... Womanism is committed to the wholeness and flourishing of the entire community." Gafney, *Womanist Midrash*, 7. Gafney further explains of her work in *Womanist Midrash* that "womanist midrash is a set of interpretive practices, including translation, exegesis, and biblical interpretation, that attends to marginalized characters in biblical narratives, especially women and girls, intentionally including and centering on non-Israelite peoples and enslaved persons.... [It] is deeply rooted in a biblical piety that respects the Scriptures as the word of God and ... a profound concern never to misrepresent the biblical texts." Gafney, *Womanist Midrash*, 3.

ingenuity and cunning of [Rebekah's] plan is itself a mark of divine guidance and her role as divine helper."[61] While Rebekah's actions as a mother may be questioned and criticized by some,

> the biblical text itself does not condemn her (Gen. 27:5–6). On the contrary, it claims that her actions are in harmony with God's plan as put forth in the oracle. . . . Surprisingly, she unfolds as the strongest figure in this narrative, towering over four men: first Eliezar, then Isaac, then her two sons, Jacob and Esau. The story of Rebecca demonstrates that the biblical mother could be a forceful personality, even within a limited and androcentric arena.[62]

Like the women who came before her, Rebekah does not fit into the boundaries of patriarchal motherhood. She chose for herself to marry her husband and chose when to travel to him, following the path laid out by Sarah and Abraham and leaving her brother Laban behind to care for their mother's house. She did not seek approval from a complementarian, "servant leader," male authority in her life to make this move. She was loved by her husband, if not protected by him, with the love he once had for his mother, Sarah, signifying lasting relational bonds. She did not seem to long for children compared to other barren mothers in the Bible, as she said nothing of that situation, and it was her husband who prayed for a child. This attitude also does not match the intensive mothering ideal that prioritizes motherhood above all else, or the complementarian ideal that does the same, only with religious backing.

When Rebekah did conceive and struggled with her pregnancy, she did not seek guidance from her husband or a religious authority but instead went straight to God. God answering her directly demonstrated that God viewed this as an appropriate action. God's answer went beyond a simple explanation, however, as Rebekah received an oracle of the future. When that future arrived, Rebekah again deemed it appropriate to act without the approval of male headship in her life; further, she took steps to work out God's plan against the wishes of her husband and oldest son. These actions fly directly in the face of the complementarian instruction that "in a well-ordered biblical marriage both husband and wife acknowledge in principle that, if necessary in some disagreement, the husband will accept the burden of making the final choice."[63] Whether or not the union between Rebekah

---

61. Frymer-Kensky, *Reading the Women*, 19.
62. Bronner, *Stories of Biblical Mothers*, 16.
63. Piper and Grudem, *Recovering Biblical Manhood*, 55.

and Isaac could be considered a "well-ordered biblical marriage," we know that it was a loving, biblical marriage. However, rather than receiving condemnation for her rebellion in acting against her husband's "burden of a final choice," Rebekah is praised for her actions both in the Bible and throughout Jewish and Christian history. The biblical takeaway here seems to be that women are empowered to make their own life choices, live with or without children, seek out God without an intermediary, receive God's words directly, and act in defiance of male authority in the interest of fulfilling God's plan for herself and her children. Rebekah's narrative overflows the boundaries of patriarchal motherhood, indeed!

LEAH, RACHEL, BILHAH, AND ZILPAH

The tradition of complicated family relationships continues with more historical examples of motherhood. This grouping of women mother those who become the twelve tribes of Israel, making them true matriarchs, although Bilhah and Zilpah were servants who were conscripted as surrogates to birth children for their mistresses Rachel and Leah. The actions of Rebekah, discussed above, catapulted her son Jacob into the world of these women when he left his home for that of his uncle in fear for his life. This is the point when the biblical reader is first introduced to Rachel. In Gen 29, Jacob traveled eastward and stopped to ask a group of shepherds about his uncle Laban; they were waiting for the remaining flocks to arrive in order to water their sheep together. Rachel led one of those flocks and appeared on the scene when the shepherds and Jacob were discussing her father, Laban.

> Rachel, the future daughter-in-law of Rebekah, was as active a matriarch as her mother-in-law, who was also her aunt. Rachel is busy shepherding her father's sheep when Jacob encounters her. This introduction is striking for many reasons. Shepherding in the Bible is a powerful and dominant metaphor for leading the people of Israel as a civil (monarch) and religious (prophet) leader and for God's own care of God's people. Civil and religious shepherding are combined in descriptions of messianic leaders in the biblical text.[64]

When Jacob saw Rachel coming, he attempted to send the shepherds away. They refused, replying that action would be outside their shepherding system; they wouldn't water their flocks until later (Gen 29:7–8).

---

64. Gafney, *Womanist Midrash*, 54.

Nevertheless, when Rachel arrived, Jacob jumped into action, uncovered the well and watered the flocks she brought with her, the flocks of her father Laban. The shepherds Jacob had been in conversation with, who were waiting to water their flocks together, are not mentioned again. Jacob apparently watered Laban's sheep without them. Following this, Jacob kissed Rachel and wept. Rachel originally had arrived unaccompanied except by sheep, expecting to interact with the other *male* shepherds. "The stereotype of biblical women being confined to the home, to women's company, avoiding the public sphere and the company of (unrelated) men, falls on its face with the introduction of Rachel in the Bible."[65] Instead of arriving to her familiar cohort of shepherds, Rachel is instead confronted with a weeping, unknown man. This man first watered her sheep and then kissed her. It was not until after this kiss that Jacob revealed who he was. Even considering the standard cultural practices concerning physical contact of the era—for example, Laban later embraced and kissed Jacob in welcome—this greeting is quite an introduction to a previously unknown relative.

Through a series of intentionally misleading events, Jacob became married to two sisters, first Leah and then the sister he loved, Rachel. While polygamy later became unlawful, that is not an issue at this time and in this context. The issue is that Laban insisted Jacob marry his older daughter Leah when Jacob loved and wished to marry Rachel instead. The reason for Leah's singleness at this point in the narrative is unclear. Leah's eyes are described as either "weak" or "lovely," depending on the translation, and she is the older of the two sisters. At this point, this is all readers know about Leah. Rachel, not Leah, is described as "graceful and beautiful" (verse 17). Even still, "Leah is not described as ugly, deformed, or blind, which may have impacted her ability to marry. As the daughter of a relatively wealthy man, Leah was a desirable bride. Nothing in the canon to this point suggests that women were chosen as potential mates based on their looks alone—however much female beauty might occasionally be celebrated in the text."[66] Laban deceived Jacob into marrying Leah rather than Rachel, justifying his actions with the explanation that custom dictated the older daughter was to be given in marriage first. While the reason Laban neglected to arrange another marriage to someone else for Leah prior to this event is unclear, what is clear is that she was an unwanted bride for Jacob. "Leah is in a horrible position. . . . Her father has used her for his own devices. She is

---

65. Gafney, *Womanist Midrash*, 55.
66. Gafney, *Womanist Midrash*, 63.

married to a man who does not love her as much as he loves her sister, if he loves her at all. For whatever reason, she entered into competition with her sister for Jacob's love."[67] As a result of this competition, she bore four sons: Reuben, Simeon, Levi, and Judah, while Rachel, like her foremothers before her, remained barren. "What is compelling here is that God . . . cares about Leah when no one else does, and gives her the one thing that will grant her status and standing in her androcentric society."[68]

Rachel, although loved by Jacob, was jealous of her sister Leah and demanded that Jacob give her children. Jacob rightly claimed that God, not himself, caused her to be childless. Rachel then pulled her servant Bilhah, who had previously been Laban's servant, into the competition, giving her to Jacob to have children. Like Hagar before her, Bilhah had no voice and no option; she must do as her mistress decided. Bilhah gave birth first to Dan and then Naphtali.[69] Unlike Sarah and Hagar, there was no rivalry between Rachel and Bilhah, and Rachel claimed Bilhah's sons as her own. The births of Bilhah's sons intensified the conflict between the sisters, and Leah pressed her servant Zilpah, who had also previously been a servant of Laban, into surrogacy; Zilpah birthed Gad and Asher. Like Bilhah, Zilpah had no voice. Like Rachel, Leah claimed her servant's sons as her own and like Rachel, Leah was the one to name these sons.

> Zilpah is presented as another pawn in the war for Jacob's attention and affection. The battlefield for that war was the bodies of Bilhah and Zilpah. Through the sexual and reproductive occupation of their bodies, people who would be known as Israel came into being. Through the wombs of Rachel, Leah, Bilhah, and Zilpah, Israel's people were birthed by choice and by force.[70]

Leah continued in her quest to gain the favor of Jacob, using the mandrakes gifted to her by her eldest son Reuben to barter with Rachel for a night with Jacob. This night resulted in her son Issachar. Leah later birthed both Zebulun and Dinah, with no mention of bartering for nights with Jacob. Although Jacob does not love Leah like he loves Rachel, he is still clearly willing to sleep with her, as he has done with Bilhah and Zilpah. It is not until after all these children that Rachel finally conceived and birthed a son,

---

67. Gafney, *Womanist Midrash*, 63.

68. Gafney, *Womanist Midrash*, 64.

69. Rachel claimed the right of the mother to name these sons. That their birth mother, Bilhah, might name them was not a consideration.

70. Gafney, *Womanist Midrash*, 63.

Joseph. Although much of this narrative has revolved around childbirth, for the first time, all women involved are now birth mothers.

After some conflict between their shared husband Jacob and their father Laban, Rachel and Leah joined Jacob in his return to the land of Canaan. An interesting event took place involving Rachel as her family was departing; Rachel secretly decided to take her father's household gods. It is clear prior to this action that both Rachel and Leah feel they have been unfairly treated by their father, claiming, "He has sold us, and he has been using up the money given for us" (Gen 31:15). Perhaps Rachel felt she was owed these gods; author Jaqueline Lapsley claims, "Rachel believes that the [household gods], whatever their precise meaning, are hers by right."[71] By the time Laban caught up with her family and began to search Rachel's tent for these gods, Rachel had "hidden them in the camel's saddle, and sat on them." She kept them concealed by saying to her father, "Let my lord not be angry that I cannot rise before you, for the way of women is upon me" (Gen 31:34–35).

Lapsley has intriguing insights into Rachel's words, highlighting their possible double meaning. She connects "I cannot rise (stand) before you" with the cultural practice of standing before one's adversary or accuser. As a woman, Rachel would not have had this right; therefore, she cannot "stand before" Laban to make her case as a man would. This inability to "stand before" her father leads to the additional double meaning of "the way of the women." A surface reading of this phrase implies menstruation, a reasonable excuse for not standing. However, as she is deprived of standing before her accuser, which could be equated with "the way of the men," she resorts to cunning, using what she has available to her to affect her will. This subversive yet clever manipulation of the situation then could be considered the "way of the women."[72] For today's reader, this portion of Rachel's story may appear tainted by her loyalty to any gods other than the true God of what will become Israel (her descendants). However, in a world prior to religious prohibitions of household gods and as a daughter who was raised in the tradition of these very gods, Rachel's agency in this narrative can be appreciated as a woman righting a wrong against herself.

The narrative continued without Rachel, Leah, Bilhah, and Zilpah at this point, including travels, tragedy, and conflict with the local people of the land. It was not until after all of this, as the family journeyed from Bethel to

---

71. Lapsley, *Whispering the Word*, 24.
72. For a full discussion on Rachel's speech, see Lapsley, *Whispering the Word*, 22–34.

Ephrath, that Rachel experienced severe labor and died shortly after giving birth to a son she named Ben-oni, but Jacob named Benjamin (Gen 35:16–19). "In later biblical tradition, ironically Rachel, who experienced great struggle with fertility, assumes a larger role than any individual mother, becoming the Mother of all Israel who weeps for her children when they go into exile. . . . Her voice rises from the dead to cry on behalf of her exiled children."[73] Later, "in Genesis 49:31, Leah's death is reported. She, not Rachel, is buried with Sarah, Abraham, Rebekah, and Isaac. In death, if not in life, Leah is finally accorded the dignity of a matriarch."[74] We have no record of Bilhah and Zilpah's deaths; they are not mentioned again once their reproductive work is completed. In death as well as in life, they remain voiceless.

How do these women compare with today's motherhood ideals? In some ways they line up; both Leah and Rachel prioritize becoming mothers. However, Leah's motivation does not seem to be to become a mother but rather to win Jacob's love. "Leah's relationship with Jacob indicates that loveless marriages, man sharing, jealousy, and competition are not just contemporary issues. There is no happy ending for Leah; she is not fulfilled as a person or as a woman in motherhood. She is not the last woman to go to her grave longing for the love of a man who does not love her but is willing to sleep with her."[75] Jacob may not have loved Leah, but God did, blessing her with children. She is also granted matriarch status. Bilhah and Zilpah are likewise unloved, and used as pawns in someone else's competition. They both represent the "woman who has had more than one abusive relationship, the woman who has been raped by more than one perpetrator, the woman who has been betrayed by women and men, the woman who has never known anyone to value her for more than what they think about her body, in part or the whole. And [they represent] the woman who survives her abuse."[76] Although often overlooked, they are both also mothers of Israel. While each of these women became mothers within a patriarchal society, their life stories do not comfortably fit within the bounds of today's traditional motherhood. These bounds are not broad enough to incorporate the unloved, the abused, the powerless, or the women who cannot keep their children. The traditional motherhood ideal is not true to life; these

---

73. Bronner, *Stories of Biblical Mothers*, 21.
74. Gafney, *Womanist Midrash*, 66.
75. Gafney, *Womanist Midrash*, 66.
76. Gafney, *Womanist Midrash*, 69.

women carry the burden of unrealistic motherhood expectations without the flexibility needed to accommodate their life situations.

Rachel, the only woman in this narrative with the love of Jacob, longs for children she is unable to have, leading to unhappiness, discord with her husband, and ugly competition with the other women involved. At the same time, she is introduced as a shepherdess, working outside the home and away from male oversight, interacting in society, including with men who are not her relatives. The shepherdess role is also reminiscent of both civil and religious leaders. This leadership was displayed when she advocated for herself after she had been wronged, badgered her husband for a child, pressed her servant into surrogacy, and bartered with her sister for mandrakes. The shepherdess role also proves to be appropriate as she metaphorically became the mother of Israel, expressing lament for her children in exile, which is a different but important kind of leadership. Like her foremothers before her, Rachel did not fulfill the role of the submissive wife and mother valued by complementarian ideology. Nor did she fulfill the role of intensive mothering, as much of her life story does not revolve around her children. She does provide a positive example of a woman who longs to mother, even eventually giving her life to give birth to her child. This grouping of women demonstrates that while the role of mother remains valid and important, much more is involved in mothers' lives, even for those whose sole longing appears to be motherhood.

HANNAH

Like Sarah, Rebekah, and Rachel before her, Hannah was a barren woman who longed to be a mother. Like Sarah, Hagar, Leah, Rachel, Bilhah, and Zilpah, Hannah was also positioned to experience conflict with a co-wife. Like Rachel, Hannah had her husband's love over and against her potential competition. Her husband Elkanah's other wife, Peninnah, had children while Hannah did not, and Peninnah used this circumstance to "provoke her severely." This situation was a long-term situation, as 1 Samuel informs us that this "went on year by year" (1:7). To make matters worse, her husband demonstrated his lack of understanding by asking, "Why do you weep? Why do you not eat? Why is your heart sad? Am I not more to you than ten sons?" (1:8). That this was not the comfort he intended it to be was demonstrated by Hannah's continued longing for a child.

"The tension develops in this part as the consequences of Hannah's childlessness, Peninnah's jealousy, and Elkanah's lack of understanding are made known. But these dynamics develop in an unexpected way because Hannah does not respond to the problematic words of her cowife or husband."[77] There was no complaining to her husband about her rival or engaging in the mistreatment of her competition as there was with Sarah and Hagar. She did not demand children of her husband as Rachel did, and she did not give servants to serve as surrogates or barter for mandrakes and nights with her shared husband as Rachel and Leah did. Instead, "She took the situation squarely into her own hands, went to the shrine, and spoke to the Lord, the only one who did not misunderstand her."[78] Hannah demonstrated faith as she turned to God in her difficult situation, making her own vow to the Lord. "Hannah's desire for a child is so desperate that she is willing to wholly dedicate him to the service of God. This distinguishes her from her barren predecessors. . . . Hannah imposes righteous standards upon herself and her offspring."[79]

It is interesting to note that in this context, Hannah employed her own agency in the matter. Her husband Elkanah demonstrated he was a devout man by worshiping and sacrificing to the Lord each year. However, in this instance, Hannah took the initiative rather than Elkanah. Unlike the situation between Jacob and Rebekah, where Jacob prayed for Rebekah to bear a child, this time, it was Hannah who presented herself to the Lord. In addition, in this situation, Hannah made her own vow. She did not seek guidance or permission from her husband; she was alone in this struggle, and she alone went to God in petition. As Joan E. Cook explains, Elkanah and Hannah would have worshiped in the context of family religion "prior to the structuring of pilgrimage festivals prescribed in the Pentateuchal legal texts. Family religion at the time probably gave men and women virtually the same roles, except for priestly eligibility which was reserved for men."[80] Even in this context, Hannah stands out as devout, a woman who wrestled with trying circumstances by seeking God rather than any other course of action.

> These actions had several conflicting implications: she looked outside her family for the support lacking within it; she took a step to achieve her social role as wife and protect her family line. But in

---

77. Cook, *Hannah's Desire*, 36.
78. Cook, *Hannah's Desire*, 50.
79. Bronner, *Stories of Biblical Mothers*, 31.
80. Cook, *Hannah's Desire*, 39.

vowing to dedicate the child to the Lord she also gave up the normal familial relationship between mother and son, thus increasing the tension in the narrative. In fact, Hannah's promise unites her purpose with that of her husband: she promises to give God her own first-fruits, like Elkanah. And her promise determines her own future as well as that of Israel. Her action marks a change in her, toward a determination and decisiveness that become her hallmark characteristics.[81]

First Samuel 1:9–10 inform the reader that Hannah "presented herself before the LORD" and prayed; as she prayed, she was deeply distressed and wept bitterly. "Was it unusual for women to come to offer their own prayers? The story doesn't hint that there was any irregularity involved. Eli, the priest, doesn't try to chase her away or tell her that women belong in the home. It is the intensity of her prayers and their long duration that attract his attention, and the fact that he cannot make out what she is saying."[82] Eli initially mistook Hannah for being drunk because of the manner of her prayers. However, her clarification resulted in an assurance from Eli that God would grant her request. In this scene, Hannah "emerges as a strong, assertive and determined barren women who dares to challenge destiny. She daringly enters the sanctuary and plaintively beseeches God for a child, assuring [God] of her devotion to raise a son in a godly manner and to dedicate [him] to lifelong service in the tabernacle."[83] This request was granted, and Hannah gave birth to a son she named Samuel. "This child is Hannah's. She has prayed for it, she has been promised it, and when the boy is born, she takes control. There is no question here of the father asserting dominance over the child: she herself names the child."[84]

After Samuel was born, Hannah again asserted her agency and did not go with her husband and his household on their annual pilgrimage to make a sacrifice and pay his vow. Instead, she kept her son at home until he was weened before returning to the shrine. Once Samuel was weened, she completed her own vow; she brought her own sacrifice in the form of a "three-year-old bull, an ephah of flour, and a skin of wine" and dedicated her son to the Lord (1 Sam 1:24). "We here learn from Hannah's experience . . . that mothers at that time had the power to dedicate their sons to holy

---

81. Cook, *Hannah's Desire*, 37.
82. Frymer-Kensky, *Reading the Women*, 304.
83. Bronner, *Stories of Biblical Mothers*, 31.
84. Frymer-Kensky, *Reading the Women*, 305.

service. There is no evidence of a father or anyone else contradicting Hannah's initial dedication to temple service."[85] While we might see her actions as abandonment, those in her context would have seen it as a sacred act.

Following this dedication, "Hannah sings a carefully crafted hymn that expresses the specific concerns of an agricultural and pastoral society in the Galilean hills.... Likewise it expresses the conviction that those who rely on the Deity will be protected and rewarded with reversals of fortune in their daily life."[86] Hannah's agency in seeking a child and her devotion in both her vow and act of dedicating her son to the Lord, is an inspiring narrative on its own. However, this narrative increases in significance as Hannah's actions are revealed as changing the course of history. These actions usher Israel into a new era of priestly reform and eventual transition to a monarchy. Her song, as does Mary's song in the New Testament at the birth of Jesus, foreshadows this new era of peace and justice.[87]

Hannah then left Samuel in the care and service of Eli, and continued to visit him. She demonstrated her ongoing faithfulness to God and her mothering care of Samuel by bringing a coat for him each year during her family's annual pilgrimage to the shrine. She was then further blessed with more children.

Overall, Bronner describes Hannah as strong, assertive, determined, and daring. Cook bestows her with determination and decisiveness and Frymer-Kensky declares she was in control. These descriptions do not reflect the "submissive wife and mother" ideology adhered to by advocates of complementarian theology. At the same time, Hannah is admired for her forbearance in dealing with her rival wife Peninnah, demonstrating strength of character in her refusal to engage when irritated and provoked. Hannah is also much admired both for her strong desire to be a mother and for her devout actions in seeking God. However much this attitude is applauded, and her desire for a child aligns with the ideals of intensive mothering, she cannot appropriately be placed within the bounds of patriarchal motherhood, complementarian motherhood, or intensive mothering. For all her notable characteristics and actions, Hannah *gave up her child* to the service of the Lord. While she does continue to demonstrate her mothering for Samuel by providing a new coat for him every year, an annual visit falls far short of the expectations placed on mothers in today's intensive

---

85. Bronner, *Stories of Biblical Mothers*, 32.
86. Cook, *Hannah's Desire*, 40.
87. Cook, *Hannah's Desire*, 40.

mothering environment. Hannah is the one mother surveyed thus far who seems to both have her own agency (unlike Hagar, Bilhah, and Zilpah) and to have done everything "right" according to Christian motherhood ideals: she longed for a child and yet she did not reach for forbidden fruit, she did not press servants into surrogacy or otherwise mistreat them, she did not manipulate, demand, compete, or barter, and she did not engage with her own tormentor. Instead, she sought God's help directly. Hannah is also the only mother who made the intentional choice not to raise her child herself, possibly making her, while admired, the mother the furthest away from today's mothering ideals.[88]

NEW TESTAMENT CONTEXT

By the New Testament era, views on women and mothers changed from what they had been during the Old Testament period. In this ancient Mediterranean world, Eve's narrative had morphed from the straightforward and relatively non-judgmental account in Genesis to a parallel of the Greco-Roman myth of Pandora. In this reimagined interpretation, Eve was considered to have brought sin into the world by eating the forbidden fruit at the tempting of a now-phallic serpent. It is essential to note in conjunction with this action that in this period, a woman's mouth was understood to be connected to her womb, as were other, more accurately connected parts of her anatomy, creating something of a parallel between them. Eve's eating of the fruit was done without the consent of Adam; Eve opened herself and allowed a forbidden substance in. Similarly, Pandora was understood to have brought chaos into the world by opening her jar, later translated as "box," without her husband's consent. This jar or box was a euphemism for her womb, bringing sexual connotations to the myth. Eve and Pandora were understood to be the cause of all sin, evil, and chaos in the previously perfect world.[89] This understanding greatly affected the everyday lives of women. "Interpretive traditions surrounding Eve and Pandora offer similar answers: Woman is a later creation from man, and while she is similar and alluring in appearance—designed to draw man to her—she ultimately

---

88. Children are adopted out for many reasons; mothers today who give their children for adoption may receive varied responses to that action, not all of them positive. However, those who have adopted out their children may find solid biblical precedent for adoption in the character of Hannah.

89. Myers, *Blessed Among Women?*, 24–30.

brings disaster as a result of her difference from the man and, especially, her unwillingness to submit to him."[90] In this context, the "warning for men to act masculine by exercising their divinely ordained control rings clear."[91]

The understanding of female anatomy in that cultural setting was also highly androcentric, to the point of being misogynistic. As explained by Alicia D. Myers, "The ancient world was a 'unisex' one. For the Greco-Roman world . . . there was really only *one* true sex/gender: the male. The female is not a unique being meriting full discussion, but rather an inverted male and useful only to highlight assumed male normativity, which is equated with his superiority."[92] In this "one sex" viewpoint, the female was understood to be a deformed male who was created by inferior sperm in the empty vessel of her mother; this inferior sperm was the fault of the man's mother or grandmother. It was believed that without regular injections of sperm to weigh it down, a woman's menstrual blood would rise to her brain, causing her to go insane, and could potentially cause so much trouble as to lead to suicide. Women were considered inferior and useless, except for the capacity to act as vessels that could carry, bear, and nurse children.[93] It was further believed that "the uterus could become untethered from its original position and move about a woman's body causing all kinds of mental illness and poor judgement."[94] Overall, "women's bodies were seen as more primitive, wetter, colder, more disorganized, and spongier. They were generally passive, especially in intelligence and in reproduction."[95]

Although today's medical knowledge has increased to the point of making the "wandering womb" and other ancient understandings of female anatomy obsolete and ridiculous, the moral and physical conclusions drawn from these ancient beliefs echo throughout history; they are still reflected in corners of today's motherhood culture. "Not only did centuries of church theologians believe that the maternal body was a sign of polluted humanity, they also believed that the pain of birthing labor was a metaphysical reality that reflected the sinfulness of women and connected every single woman back to the disobedient and rebellious Eve."[96] In the ancient world,

---

90. Myers, *Blessed Among Women?*, 30.
91. Myers, *Blessed Among Women?*, 30.
92. Myers, *Blessed Among Women?*, 19.
93. Myers, *Blessed Among Women?*, 31–38.
94. Marga, *In the Image*, 44.
95. Marga, *In the Image*, 45.
96. Marga, *In the Image*, 13.

motherhood effectively demonstrated [women's] recognition of inferiority beneath their men, as well as their acceptance of the maternal telos prescribed for them. Yet, the public displays of maternal submission . . . also offered select women increased agency through the recognition of their feminine virtue. . . . Moreover, men who fathered legitimate children through their wives likewise demonstrated their own virtue—that is, their masculinity—by controlling the weaker feminine and purposing her for her "natural," maternal, end. . . . "Real" women were mothers, and "real" men made them.[97]

Today as well as in the ancient world, motherhood offers women acceptance and recognition of their "feminine virtue," designating those who are mothers as the "real women" in society. Thankfully, the viewpoint that a woman's value lies primarily in her ability to bear children is no longer mainstream, even if shadows of this point of view and hints of viewing women as inferior are persistently a part of today's not-quite-egalitarian society. Some of these shadows are also revealed in the fact that women's health can be neglected, and pregnancies are increasingly dangerous in this century. While the extreme versions of the ideology of personal worth based on birthing children are rare, this extremity *was* the culture of the ancient world in which New Testament events occurred and the culture in which these events were interpreted and recorded.

MARY

While the Old Testament records several examples of women giving astonishing births, indicating divine intent for the children being born, none of these accounts compare to the miraculous birth experienced by Mary the mother of Jesus. Although the pregnancies of Sarah, Rebekah, Rachel, and Hannah were unexpected because of their barrenness and only accomplished with the direct intervention of God, Mary's situation was altogether different in that she was not barren but rather young, engaged but not yet married, betrothed but still virginal. Luke 1:27 states that Mary was "a virgin engaged to a man whose name was Joseph." The customs of the ancient world suggest that she would have been young enough to be considered a child bride by today's standards. "The Jewish betrothal practice took place before a girl reached twelve and a half. Therefore, as a virgin, Mary would

---

97. Myers, *Blessed Among Women?*, 7.

have been a young girl of marriageable age without the benefit of sexual intercourse,"[98] perhaps even too young to naturally conceive. This is significant. As Edward Sri explains, "To note that Mary is betrothed and then say she is a virgin is, in a sense, redundant. So why does Luke mention Mary being a virgin—and not just once, but twice in one verse? He does so in order to draw attention to her virginity in a unique way, as it will play a key part of the story as it unfolds."[99] Mary's virginal state will be offered as proof that this child will be the son of God, not a son of man, carried in the empty "vessel" of Mary.

"The angel Gabriel was sent by God" (1:26), to bring a message to Mary. He begins with, "Greetings, favored one!" This term, "favored one," is "traditionally translated 'full of grace'" and "gives us a window into a profound spiritual gift God gave her."[100] Sri notes that Mary is the only person in Scripture to receive this title, explaining, "It becomes clear that Mary stands out in all of salvation history, underscoring the unique divine favor bestowed on her."[101] God is seen as blessing Mary in a unique way in preparation to bear God's son Jesus. Gabriel follows this greeting with, "The Lord is with you" (1:28). This phrase has precedent in the Old Testament and is significant in its use here.

"All throughout the Old Testament, the message is clear. The expression 'the Lord is with you' is used when God summons someone to a formidable task in [God's] saving plan. The person is going to be stretched like never before and will need to rely on God like never before. That's why God or the angel offers the divine assurance that they are not alone in their mission."[102] As will be demonstrated, this was certainly the case with Mary.

After this introduction, the angel Gabriel then shares that Mary will bear a child, who will be the "Son of the Most High" and will "reign over the house of Jacob forever" (1:31–33). These are grandiose claims for someone who would be born to Mary, considered to be part of the "pious poor."[103] However, Mary's initial concern is more immediate. She asks, "How can this be, since I am a virgin?" (1:34). Gabriel's answer—"The Holy Spirit will come

---

98. Buckhanon Crowder, *When Momma Speaks*, ch. 7.
99. Sri, *Rethinking Mary*, 4.
100. Sri, *Rethinking Mary*, 23.
101. Sri, *Rethinking Mary*, 25.
102. Sri, *Rethinking Mary*, 31.
103. McKnight, *Jesus Creed*, 85.

upon you, and the power of the Most High will overshadow you" (1:35)—is rich with meaning:

> Luke's description of the Holy Spirit coming upon Mary recalls the creative activity of God's Spirit at the creation of the cosmos (Gn 1:2; Ps 33:6) and in the creation of individuals (Jb 33:4; Ps 104:30; Jdt 16:14). Luke is underscoring how what's happening in Mary with the conception of her child is completely the work of God—a new creation. As Brown notes, the Spirit that comes upon Mary brings to mind "the Spirit of God that hovered over the waters before creation in Gen 1:2. The earth was void and without form when that Spirit appeared; just so Mary's womb was a void until the Spirit of God filled it with a child who was His Son."[104]

Further, "Luke is making an important point about Mary. She is the first disciple to receive the gift of the Spirit, anticipating what other faithful disciples will receive. She goes before the other disciples who will receive this gift after Jesus's Death, Resurrection, and Ascension."[105] Mary, who contributed her humanity to the incarnation, was not left alone in her humanity. God prepared her with divine grace, assured her of divine presence, and sent her the Holy Spirit.

Mary's unexpected pregnancy not only included being "overshadowed" by the power of the Most High, it also included the *exclusion* of Joseph, her husband-to-be. Interestingly, this contrasts the pronouncement in Genesis stating, "Your turning is to your man/husband, and he shall rule/control you [sexually]."[106] It was also counter-cultural in a society where men held power, and impregnating their wives was a sign of their masculine virtue:

> Her response to Gabriel relativizes, even places in jeopardy, her pending marriage to Joseph and her place in his household—both because she has agreed to a pregnancy apart from the honor and security of marriage and because she has declared her primary and ultimate allegiance to God rather than to a life of subservience to her husband-to-be. For her, partnership in the aims of God transcends the claims of family.[107]

---

104. Sri, *Rethinking Mary*, 58. Sri's quotation of Raymond Brown comes from Brown, *Birth of the Messiah*, 314.
105. Sri, *Rethinking Mary*, 60.
106. Meyers, *Rediscovering Eve*, 102.
107. Gaventa and Rigby, *Blessed One*, 15.

Jesus will reinforce this allegiance to God over the claims of family later in her life. Further, "well before Joseph knows that Mary is pregnant, Mary is told by the angel Gabriel that she is to conceive supernaturally. Mary instantaneously grasps what this means: She will be labeled in her community as a *na'ap* (adulteress). The label is inaccurate, but it sticks."[108] Mary did not "turn to her husband" for pregnancy or prioritize her family or her submissive family role in a culture in which it was dangerous not to, and she accepted the inaccurate slander that was sure to result. In the face of these cultural and practical considerations,

> Mary's response "Here am I, the servant of the Lord. Let it be with me according to your word"—is . . . a free, strong, and courageous response . . . and has nothing to do with what is commonly understood by words like passivity and servility. Mary does not submit to coercion; she freely consents to the working of God's grace in and through her. That her consent is not made without deliberation and struggle is hinted by Mary's question, "How can this be?" Far from being a mere puppet, Mary makes an active, conscious, and free choice to participate in God's destiny for her.[109]

This agency is emphasized by Leclerc and Peterson who share that "Mary's empowerment by the Spirit shows her as more than a passive vessel or womb,"[110] describing her instead as "independent, intentional, and active in her obedience and discipleship. . . . She is like the Christ in her independent and willful obedience, and in her empowerment through the same Spirit that is in Christ."[111] They also point out that the early church father Irenaeus makes a fascinating parallel in his doctrine of recapitulation. Just as Christ is the Second Adam (Rom 5) by obeying God when Adam did not, he also says that Mary recapitulates Eve's sin through Mary's active and willing positive response to what God asks of her. We understand that Paul's use of the Second Adam is intended to imply that as we are in Christ, we, too, can live a life of full obedience. Irenaeus clearly intends that Christian women and mothers are to live like Mary in her positive response to God. Mary sets an example for women and men alike in this regard.[112]

---

108. McKnight, *Jesus Creed*, 85.
109. Gaventa and Rigby, *Blessed One*, 123–24.
110. Leclerc and Peterson, *Side of the Cross*, 65.
111. Leclerc and Peterson, *Side of the Cross*, 64.
112. Leclerc and Peterson, *Side of the Cross*, 62–65.

As with the barren women of the Old Testament, God was again involved in the birthing process, this time doing something that had not been done before; Mary would become a mother not by a patriarch or prophet but by God. It is also interesting to note that Mary visited her cousin Elizabeth while she was expecting. Elizabeth is another woman who remained barren until her old age, then became pregnant with God's intervention. Cook points out a beautiful progression in the pairs of biblical women who struggled with fertility: Sarah mistreated Hagar, Rachel and Leah bitterly competed, Hannah persevered under Peninnah's provocation, and Elizabeth and Mary related to each other with warmth and blessing.[113] "Mary is fortunate in that as a pregnant teenager she is able to spend time with a sister-mother-girlfriend figure who consoles and counsels her for three months. She, who lacks much social and political privilege, has the gift of having someone walk with her through the first trimester of her pregnancy."[114] That she was able to make this visit and share this support is also somewhat unusual since "within her social world, Mary has a script to follow. This script would involve her relative seclusion, not a journey of some seventy miles (no chaperone or traveling companions are mentioned by Luke!), and her submission to her father or husband, not her purposeful resolve."[115] Mary, now blessed with grace, God's presence, the Holy Spirit, and carrying Jesus in her womb, was again unconcerned with social convention. She visited her cousin Elizabeth who was experiencing her miraculous pregnancy.

When Mary arrived to greet Elizabeth, Elizabeth's child "leaped in her womb," Elizabeth "was filled with the Holy Spirit" herself, and she exclaimed about Mary, "Blessed are you among women, and blessed is the fruit of your womb" (Luke 1:42) According to Sri, only two other women throughout Scripture were designated with this title, both called blessed for their acts in defeating their enemies.[116] These other women "helped liberate the people from pagan armies. Mary's child will save Israel from a much more dangerous enemy. . . . Mary's child will save the people from

---

113. Cook, *Hannah's Desire*, 97.
114. Buckhanon Crowder, *When Momma Speaks*, 79.
115. Gaventa and Rigby, *Blessed One*, 15.
116. Sri cites Jael in Judg 5:24–26 and the apocryphal Judith in Jdt 13:18. Jael overcomes her enemy by pounding a tent peg through his head, and Judith overcomes hers by cutting off his head with a sword. Sri, *Rethinking Mary*, 73.

their sins (see Lk 1:77)."[117] The reader is also reminded of another enemy foreshadowed in Gen 3:15. This passage claims that an offspring of Eve's will strike the head of the serpent. The serpent is represented here as the ultimate enemy found in the person of the devil. Mary "is the 'woman' whose son will defeat the devil as Genesis 3:15 foretold."[118] At the same time, to "recognize Mary's blessedness, then, should not mean we elevate her to superhuman status. . . . Instead, to say Mary is the 'Blessed One' is to join with the Spirit of the Magnificat, to prophesy about who God is and what God has done. Mary is the Blessed One because of what God has done in her and through her."[119]

Elizabeth's Spirit-filled proclamation transitions in verse 46 to Mary's song, the Magnificat. Mary was part of the "pious poor," or the *Anawim*; as such, Mary's people yearned for: (1) justice; (2) the end of oppression; and (3) the coming of the Messiah.[120] "Each of these characteristics . . . finds expression in the life of Mary and especially in the *Magnificat*."[121] Mary's song echoed the beautiful hymn sung by Hannah and expressed the concerns not only of herself but also of her people. "Mary's song of praise resembles the Song of Hannah in several ways: its introduction refers explicitly to her personal receipt of divine favor, and names divine deeds on behalf of specific vulnerable groups," clarifying God acts specifically "to honor the promise to Israel's earliest ancestors and all their descendants, thereby including the Jewish community of her own day."[122] Further, both, "Samuel and Jesus, would usher in new eras of justice. Their mothers' hymns voiced that hope and celebrated that promise."[123] With this hymn, Mary added the role of "prophet"[124] to her role as "blessed one." Her prophetic voice still proclaims today, "What God has done for Mary, he is going to do for the rest of his people. The Magnificat is thus not just about blessings for Mary. It's about the blessings starting to fall on all the faithful."[125]

---

117. Sri, *Rethinking Mary*, 74.
118. Sri, *Rethinking Mary*, 74.
119. Gaventa and Rigby, *Blessed One*, 5.
120. McKnight, *Jesus Creed*, 85.
121. McKnight, *Jesus Creed*, 85.
122. Cook, *Hannah's Desire*, 99–100.
123. Cook, *Hannah's Desire*, 114.
124. Gaventa and Rigby, *Blessed One*, 54.
125. Sri, *Rethinking Mary*, 98.

Mary traveled with Joseph, who was by then her husband, to Bethlehem, carrying the Son of God in her womb. While there, she gave birth in the humblest circumstances, wrapped her newborn in cloths, and laid him in a manger.

> Of all the details Luke could report, he chooses to focus on how the child was "wrapped" in swaddling clothes and laid in a manger. Luke uses these two verbs back-to-back only one other time in his entire Gospel: at the end of Jesus's life when he was taken down from the Cross. Just as Jesus at the start of his life was wrapped in bands of cloth and laid in a manger (Lk 2:7), so too at the end of his life he was wrapped in a linen cloth and laid in a tomb after being crucified on Calvary (Lk 23:53).[126]

Sri uses this language of Jesus being wrapped in cloth to connect the Christmas event of Jesus's birth to the Good Friday event of Jesus's crucifixion: "Jesus enters the world in conditions of poverty, humility, and rejection, pointing to how he will leave this world."[127]

Although there was much fanfare amongst shepherds, angels, and wise men, Mary was now a (married) teenage mother, learning to care for her first child. A short time later, Mary and Joseph brought baby Jesus to the temple in Jerusalem to present him to the Lord. While there, Simeon prophesied over him. This prophecy recognized that God's four-hundred-year silence had now been broken in the person of Jesus, revealing God's glory and that this would cause great opposition (Luke 2:32). This opposition will also pierce Mary's soul (Luke 2:35).[128] Simeon's prophecy was a "foreshadowing of the suffering Mary will endure when her son dies on the Cross."[129]

There are varying opinions regarding Mary and her other children. Many affirm that Mary remained a virgin the entirety of her life and her other children are either Joseph's from a previous marriage, adopted, or cousins of Jesus. Others affirm that they were Mary's natural-born children, fathered by Joseph.[130] "What is important here is that, whichever view one takes, each agrees that Mary assumes responsibility for these children."[131] Mary is mother, not only to Jesus but also to his siblings.

126. Sri, *Rethinking Mary*, 109.
127. Sri, *Rethinking Mary*, 109.
128. For a full discussion on this passage, see Sri, *Rethinking Mary*, 121–35.
129. Sri, *Rethinking Mary*, 134.
130. McKnight, *Jesus Creed*, 88.
131. McKnight, *Jesus Creed*, 88.

It was some twelve years before we again saw Mary interact with her son Jesus in the biblical text. At this point, the family had traveled together in a group to Jerusalem for the Feast of the Passover. After the feast and a partial return, Mary and Joseph realized Jesus was not in their caravan. After searching for three days, they finally found him at the temple. Mary's words to Jesus after they found him in the temple—"Why have you treated us like this? Look, your father and I have been searching for you in great anxiety" (Luke 2:48)—communicates the "real and present terror of parents who do not know where their child is."[132] "Mary's comment to Jesus . . . portrays her in the role of mother, a mother whose search is accompanied by nothing less than anguish."[133] Jesus gives her an answer that neither she nor Joseph understands: "Did you not know that I must be in my Father's house?" (Luke 2:49). "In pursuing his Father's will, Jesus does some things that cause Mary pain, and she does not understand. Mary is being challenged to relate to her Son in a new way as she is confronted more directly with his mission to do his Heavenly Father's will."[134]

The conversation in the temple is followed by Jesus obediently going home to Nazareth with his parents and Mary treasuring or pondering "all these things in her heart" (Luke 2:51). This could be understood to convey "increasing misunderstanding and confusion during his childhood. . . . Mary seems to take on more of the traits of other characters in Luke's Gospel the farther away from her pregnancy she is mentioned."[135] However, rather than increased confusion, the "astonishing realism of the biblical picture of Mary reaches its peak . . . [when describing] Mary's confusion and her need for deeper understanding. . . . Mary is exemplary of the church not despite but because she is portrayed in Scripture as being a person of faith who must learn the meaning of Christian discipleship through obedience and who must remain open to reform."[136] In fact, Gaventa and Rigby assert, "If the gospels had depicted John the Baptist or Peter pondering over Jesus, the 'church would long ago have dubbed these as moments of theological reflection.' Maybe it is time to consider them thus."[137]

---

132. Gaventa, *Mary*, 68.
133. Gaventa, *Mary*, 68.
134. Sri, *Rethinking Mary*, 142.
135. Myers, *Blessed Among Women?*, 65.
136. Gaventa and Rigby, *Blessed One*, 125.
137. Gaventa, *Mary*, 130; Gaventa and Rigby, *Blessed One*, 106.

Mary appeared next at a wedding both she and Jesus were attending. The setting and events of this scene place Jesus in the world of humanity, with a mother, brothers, and social events to participate in.[138] The hosts ran out of wine, and Mary reported this to Jesus. His response to her—"Woman, what does that have to do with us? My hour has not yet come" (John 2:4)—has been the recipient of confusion; Jesus's words to Mary appear difficult. However, "Mary seems to interpret Christ's words so positively that she confidently believes he is going to fulfill her request. . . . Moreover, Jesus's own actions indicate that he looks with favor on Mary's appeal for . . . he supplies more wine than Mary or anyone at the feast would have imagined."[139]

There is potentially more to this interaction, as this is the first of Jesus's miracles and launches his public ministry. According to Sri, Jesus's response to Mary could be understood as, "*My hour* has not yet come. But if I do perform this miracle to provide the wine, then the clock starts ticking on my hour—the story is set in motion and my movement toward my Passion and Death begins. . . . Are you ready for that? Is this what you want?"[140] Mary may not have understood the full import of this question; how could she? However, she was still Mary, the blessed one, overshadowed by the Spirit, prophetic singer of the Magnificat, recipient of the hard words of Simeon, the one who carried, birthed, and raised Jesus, and continued to ponder these things in her heart. This same Mary "doesn't hesitate. She continues to say yes to God's will at Cana. . . . She turns to the servants and says, 'Do whatever he tells you' (Jn 2:5)."[141]

Mary appeared again when she and Jesus's brothers could not reach him because of the crowd. Jesus's response in Luke 8:21—"My mother and my brothers are those who hear the word of God and do it"—indicates Jesus's reorienting of family and relationships. In this scenario, "Jesus insists that all other responsibilities and relationships be subordinated to faithfulness to God's word. This redefinition reaches even to notions of family, where kinship is defined not with reference to blood ties but on the basis of hearing and doing the word of God."[142] In Matt 10:37, Jesus even goes so far as to state that "whoever loves father or mother more than me is

---

138. Gaventa and Rigby, *Blessed One*, 49.
139. Sri, *Rethinking Mary*, 154.
140. Sri, *Rethinking Mary*, 164 (emphasis in original).
141. Sri, *Rethinking Mary*, 164.
142. Gaventa and Rigby, *Blessed One*, 16.

not worthy of me; and whoever loves son or daughter more than me is not worthy of me." Sri is quick to remind us that this redefinition of family does not need to exclude Mary. In fact, she was the first to "hear the word of God and do it" (Luke 8:21) when she heard God's words through the angel Gabriel and responded in faith.[143] Although Jesus's response includes all people and not only mothers, we are also reminded that Jesus "is engaged in cultural critique at this juncture in the narrative, calling into question one of the primary means by which women would have found honor in the world about which Luke writes and within which Luke's narrative would be read."[144] Mary, who had historically acted in counter-cultural ways, now found herself faced with a holy son engaged in drastically counter-cultural actions and teachings.

This redefinition of the family is reinforced when Mary is in the heart-breaking position near the foot of the cross. At this point, Jesus instructs her, "Behold, your son!" To his beloved disciple, he instructs, "Behold, your mother!" (John 19:26–27). This "results in a formal shift of kinship ties for Jesus's mother. She is no longer in her former household, which included other sons of her own (2:12; 7:1–9), but in the household of the Beloved Disciple. Her transition seems to indicate the beginning of a new familial network based on Jesus's word rather than blood ties."[145] Mary, mother of God, is also a follower of Jesus, part of the newly created "family of God," in which her membership is based not on her birthing Jesus (or anyone else) but on her willingness to "hear the word of God and do it" (Luke 8:21). "When Jesus' mother and the Beloved Disciple are given to one another and depart the scene, Jesus' connections to earthly existence likewise depart from John's gospel. Her role in this incident, then, has to do with Jesus' separation from his own earthly life."[146]

Jesus may have separated from "his own earthly life," but those familiar with the Christian faith know that this is not the end of the story for Jesus, and the same is true for Mary. While she is not definitively referenced in the resurrection account or Jesus's appearances to his disciples, it is clear she has at the least been informed, and she believes. Acts 1:14 records, "All these were constantly devoting themselves to prayer, together with certain women, including Mary the mother of Jesus, as well as his brothers." As

---

143. Sri, *Rethinking Mary*, 220.
144. Gaventa and Rigby, *Blessed One*, 12.
145. Myers, *Blessed Among Women?*, 67–68.
146. Gaventa and Rigby, *Blessed One*, 50.

Sri observes, "This verse is the last time Mary's name appears in the New Testament. And the final image of Mary on earth is one of prayer and communion. Luke presents Mary at prayer and at one with the disciples, at the center of the church, awaiting the coming of the Spirit at Pentecost."[147] The anticipation builds at this point because the reader recognizes the "same Holy Spirit that overshadowed Mary is about to be poured out on Jesus's disciples and the 3,000 people who are baptized at Pentecost (Acts 2)."[148] At this point, the Christian church will be born, and we are assured that she contributed as she joined with the other disciples in the upper room, devoted to prayer.[149]

Mary, full of grace, blessed, assured of God's presence, and overshadowed by the Holy Spirit, becomes a virginal "unwed mother." She accepts this situation with joy, although she knows she will be slandered for it. She acts counter-culturally, submitting to God rather than her father or Joseph, is active in her own decisions, and is described as "free, strong, courageous."[150] She flaunts convention in her travels, acts as a prophet, and receives a prophecy about a sword that will pierce her soul. Although she is anguished at losing her son and challenged through this experience, she ponders as a theologian; she is a disciple. She makes requests of Jesus and directs others to "do whatever [Jesus] says." She is the mother of God; she is also a mother to other children. She understands her family to be counter-culturally reoriented around the new family of God. She prays with and as one of the disciples and is part of the experience and the ushering in of the birth of the Christian church.

It seems hardly worth mentioning that Mary does not fit within the bounds of patriarchal motherhood and borders on flagrant disrespect to suggest the possibility. Her counter-cultural tendencies to flout social convention were no small matter, but they were the side effects, not the cause, of her determined actions. As a prophet, a theologian, a disciple, and yes, as a mother, she sought God and learned to seek God above all else, including family and whatever cultural ideals were attached to the familial system. Today's mother may find different cultural ideals attached to the current family system than Mary did in her day, but the principle remains the same.

---

147. Sri, *Rethinking Mary*, 228.
148. Sri, *Rethinking Mary*, 229.
149. Sri, *Rethinking Mary*, 230.
150. Gaventa and Rigby, *Blessed One*, 124.

Mothers in Christian Scripture

From Mary and the other women of the Bible who followed God, we learn that what matters most in the life of a Christian mother, a mother who follows God, is not intensive or complementarian mothering. Eve co-created with God, the first mother to both birth and mourn children. Sarah attempted an alternative path to motherhood, laughed when she learned of her impending pregnancy, then mothered with a fierceness that resulted in the oppression of others. Hagar's involuntary motherhood resulted in her mistreatment, the near-death of her son, two separate personal encounters with God, and her eventual emancipation, becoming the mother of nations herself. Rebekah, as a mother, received an oracle from God before her children were born, then used the resources available to her to orchestrate that oracle into reality. Leah and Rachel competed in motherhood, and Bilhah and Zilpah were caught up in the fray. Hannah demonstrated faith and perseverance in her quest to become a mother, dedicating her firstborn son to God. Mary received a heavenly visitation, gave a miraculous virgin birth, used her prophetic voice, raised her holy son while learning to be a disciple herself, experienced the sorrow of his persecution and death, then lived as a true disciple in the redefined family of God. The mothers of the Bible represent many and varied life circumstances, including barrenness, oppression, homelessness, loss, privilege, single parenting, adoption, child brides, power plays, mixed families, incest, competition, support, blessing, discipleship, and repeated intervention of God. Whatever circumstances today's mother faces, there is likely a biblical parallel.

As followers of God in all circumstances, "traditional family structures are neither established as Christian nor are they abandoned as obsolete; they are instead (re)shaped by the death of Jesus who honors what society shames and dismisses what the world around him most honors."[151] While what matters most in the life of a Christian mother is not intensive or complementarian mothering, it may include seeking to have a child or praying for a child. It may include fighting for, protecting, or providing for a child or a mother sacrificing her own life to give birth to a child. It may include giving a child away as Hannah did or learning to let go as Mary progressively let go of Jesus. It will likely include character traits that do not reflect complementarian or intensive mothering ideals, as modeled by the biblical mothers discussed above. It will likely overflow the bounds of patriarchal motherhood, as it did for these same biblical mothers. Finally, it will hopefully include understanding that a biological, earthly family does not equal God's family. As this

---

151. Gaventa and Rigby, *Blessed One*, 40.

overview of biblical mothers demonstrates, mothering is important but what matters most in the life of a Christian mother is not mothering at all and what matters most is not defined by how a woman mothers. Instead, as Jesus taught and as Mary discovered, what matters most in the life of a Christian mother is to hear the word of God and do it.

3

Biblical Metaphors of God as Mother

MARIA SETTLED INTO THE antique rocking chair handed down from her grandmother, tucking her three-month-old infant into place to breastfeed. Although at 2:00 a.m. she was half asleep, she appreciated the quiet house, resting her head back on the chair and soaking in the peace. She was exhausted, of course, but it made her happy that she could care for her baby, and she cherished what was to come. She knew that once her child had a full tummy, he would drift off to sleep, completely content, safe, and satisfied. She remembered the half-smile of her infant after the feeding earlier that night, with a drop of milk dribbled on his chubby cheek. She thought of this stage as "milk-drunk," and she was proud she could provide that for him.

This picture of total trust and contentment reminded her of the verse she and her husband had discovered several months back before this second child of theirs had been born. Psalm 131:2 reads, "But I have calmed and quieted my soul, like a weaned child with its mother; my soul is like the weaned child with me." Luis had shared that this verse was helping him, saying this imagery provided "an inner safe place" for him while he dealt with past trauma. Maria struggled with trauma from her past, too, both of them damaged by the figure of authority their respective fathers represented. It was the childhood containing mental and emotional abuse that Maria struggled with. However, she knew Luis's past contained mental, emotional, and physical abuse at the hands of his father. Maria's dad had disappeared from her life just as she was becoming a teenager; Luis's had passed away a year prior. This death was the event that prompted Luis to seek therapy.

Luis shared that his therapist asked about his vision of God in one session. To clarify her question, she wondered how Luis, a former pastor in a Christian church, addressed God when he began to pray. He answered, "Lord, Jesus, or God." She then asked if he ever used the term "Father," which was when he realized that he wasn't capable of addressing God in that way, even when his therapist invited him to do so. He had laughed at himself, sharing that his response was stupid, although Maria didn't think it was. He knew it was "just a prayer," but he still couldn't do it; he couldn't pray this way and have it come from his heart. Luis shared with his therapist and then later with Maria that he realized that he had been hiding from God for his entire life. Even his foray into pastoral ministry was an attempt to "like God more." Part of his workaholism and eventual burnout stemmed from his attempts to please God and avoid punishment, represented as a literal hell. Luis said he was "trying to be enough—as a senior pastor!" and followed this with a self-deprecating laugh. Although Maria was not a pastor, she realized that she also struggled with prayer and that she had often attempted to "earn" God's approval.

Another time, one of Luis's pastor friends asked if he had a different image he could use for God throughout this process. Maria remembered discussing this with Luis, and they had decided that "nature" was a good image to use. However, in a follow-up conversation with them, this friend eventually asked if they had ever considered addressing God as Mother. They had not, and Luis shared with their friend that this idea was "a no-go" in their conservative church's theology. However, they began looking in the Bible for imagery connected to "God as Mother" and discovered many verses with feminine metaphors for God, including mothering images. When they came across Ps 131:1–2, it sunk in deep, possibly because they were in the life stage of having children. It seemed as meaningful to Luis as it was to Maria; she knew he meditated on it often. This human image of contentment enriched their understanding of God, providing, in Luis's words, "an inner safe place while dealing with the trauma." Maria smiled at this memory and shifted their baby to her shoulder, patting his back briefly before readjusting him to feed on the other side. She needed that safe space to process as well.

Biblical Metaphors of God as Mother

Maria then reflected on the risk they had taken, especially Luis as an ordained minister, with their understanding of God as Mother. Although they had found support for this idea in the Bible, their church did not support this understanding. They knew that labels such as "liberal," "feminist," or "woke" could be hurled in their direction from their congregation—each a highly negative label in their conservative denomination. This was only intensified by the machismo prevalent in their culture—a great and mighty "Father God" could never be female. Maria understood now, in a way she had not before, that the deep reverence for Mary, the mother of Christ, among the Catholics of their community partially stemmed from this same need for a divine mother image. Protestants like themselves did not have this same indulgence when it came to the Holy Virgin, but thankfully, the Bible made it clear they did not need it.

Although Luis now worked in a non-profit rather than pastoring a church, Maria worried about his future ministry. However, she understood that his deep pain pushed him past the point of caring what others thought, including caring about the opinions of their denominational leadership regarding "God as Mother." He had shared that inside, he felt like he was dying; for him, it was either approach God as Mother or leave God altogether. Although he had been trying to detach his traumatic memories from his understanding of God, he couldn't find the inner safety he needed to be able to heal within the image of God as Father. Maria knew that for people with "father trauma," understanding God as Mother could be lifesaving.

As Maria stared with loving but sleepy eyes at her now "milk-drunk," peaceful little one, she conceded that God was neither mother nor father. Still, she knew that understanding God as Mother was what they had each needed. Maria knew that Luis still cherished his understanding of God as Mother, just as she cherished her growing understanding that her intense love for their baby paled compared to God's mothering love for them.

Maria's and Luis's experience notwithstanding, through most of Christian history God has been depicted as a father; this metaphor, so commonly used within the Christian church, however, has been misunderstood as more than a metaphor. Many take this literally; Christians often view God as a literal male father.[1] Further, "many people need to think of God in male terms because they do not think women or mothers are powerful

---

1. It was at the Council of Nicaea in 325 when father-son language was "standardized." Prior to Nicaea, there are many church fathers who write using a more fluid sense of gender and direct female metaphors for God, even for Jesus, e.g., Clement of Alexandria. E.g., see "Who Is the Rich Man That Shall Be Saved?" 37 (*ANF* 2:601).

enough to be in charge."[2] Where does this leave the large population of Christians who are female? If both female and male reflect the image of God (Gen 1:27), where is the female image found? "If women are created in the image of God, then God can be spoken of in female metaphors in as full and as limited a way as God is imaged in male ones, without talk of feminine dimensions reducing the impact of this imagery."[3]

For those looking for models, for examples of themselves in Christian thought and specifically in Scripture, where do they turn?[4] "A God who is father, not mother, risks being lopsided, and potentially unavailable to those people who most need to experience divine love. Such a God would be available more easily and richly to some than to others."[5] There are also those whose understanding of fathers has been marred through abuse or ill-treatment by human fathers and father figures. As a result, some who have experienced this kind of abuse cannot access or connect with positive, paternal metaphors of God. While we understand God as Father, can we also understand God as Mother? If God is viewed only as Father, and Scriptures are viewed as containing only paternal metaphors, this leaves readers with an incomplete picture of God and the Christian faith. Further, for those women who grapple with unrealistic motherhood ideals, are there Christian ideals they are called to instead? The biblical mothers referenced in the previous chapter offer evidence of this call. Leviticus 19:2 records Moses sharing God's words: "You shall be holy, for I the LORD your God am holy." This instruction is repeated several times in Leviticus[6] and in 1 Pet 1:15–16.[7] Are Christians to understand this holiness, which

---

2. Japinga, *Feminism and Christianity*, 59.

3. Johnson, *She Who Is*, 54.

4. "An early Christian tradition developed of viewing Mary as a royal figure worthy of our honor.... From a biblical perspective, Christians seeking Mary's intercession makes perfect sense. If she is our queen mother as the New Testament reveals she is, then it is most fitting that we would lovingly turn to her with our needs." Sri, *Rethinking Mary*, 81. As Sri's comment suggests, many seeking examples of the feminine in the divine have turned to the biblical Mary. However, to "recognize Mary's blessedness ... should not mean we elevate her to superhuman status.... Mary is the Blessed One because of what God has done in her and through her." Gaventa and Rigby, *Blessed One*, 9.

5. Bulkeley, *Not Only a Father*, 8.

6. See Lev 11:45; 19:2; and 20:26.

7. A call to holiness could also potentially be termed an "unrealistic ideal." However, those in the Wesleyan tradition understand holiness to mean an inner state of purity, living without intentional sin, including an eradication of original sin, "heart holiness," and that heart holiness is possible through the continual work of God's Spirit in a believer's

all Christians are to model, as expressed exclusively in male terms? As paternal metaphors enrich the Christian community for those both female and male, might not maternal metaphors do the same? What metaphors of mothering do we find in Scripture?

NUMBERS 11:12

"Did I conceive all this people? Did I give birth to them, that you should say to me, 'Carry them in your bosom, as a nurse carries a sucking child, to the land that you promised on oath to their ancestors?'" The context of this verse is of the Israelites in the desert demanding meat and other foods from Moses. Moses is not up to the task and questions God in an accusatory fashion. "Evidently Moses, like ancient Near Eastern society, sees feeding as mothers' work. The mother, who conceived and gave birth should now carry and nurse Israel. . . . Verse 12 talks of 'becoming pregnant' (*harah*) and 'giving birth' (*yalad*). It also pictures suckling, so in every way this verse is explicitly motherly."[8] Moses, when the people are pressing this role, objects. "The implication of the text is that the people are [God's] responsibility: [God] conceived this people, [God] gave birth to them, [God] is their mother."[9] Moses struggles with his leadership role, but he views "mother" as an appropriate role/metaphor for God. "That this notion is taken seriously by God is proven by the sequel, in which God responds positively to Moses' predicament."[10] God is revealed here as Mother, caring for both Moses and the people, broadening the understanding of how the divine interacts with God's people.

---

life, often termed a second act of grace. For a full statement on holiness, see Church of the Nazarene, *Manual*, part II. This sets up the potential conflict for a Christian mother between the call of society's standards, expressed through intensive/complementarian motherhood, and the call of God to heart holiness, a call extended by God to all people, including Christian mothers.

8. Bulkeley, *Not Only a Father*, 25.
9. Dille, *Mixing Metaphors*, 138.
10. Van Wijk-Bos, *Reimagining God*, 59.

ISAIAH 42:13–15

> The Lord goes forth like a soldier,
> like a warrior he stirs up his fury;
> he cries out, he shouts aloud,
> he shows himself mighty against his foes.
> For a long time I have held my peace,
> I have kept still and restrained myself;
> now I will cry out like a woman in labor,
> I will gasp and pant.
> I will lay waste mountains and hills,
> and dry up all their herbage;
> I will turn the rivers into islands,
> and dry up the pools.

Isaiah 42:13–15 presents an unusual pairing of metaphors: God as a warrior and God as a woman in labor. While the two may seem to have nothing in common, they work together within the passage to form a powerful picture of God. In fact, the "image of God as a woman in labor interacts with that of the Divine Warrior. Areas of overlap include 'crying out,' anguish, courage, danger, inevitability, the hope of deliverance from death, life, and the literary convention of one facing a siege reacting 'like a woman in labor.'"[11] Building on this, both the warrior and the woman in labor express their experience with sounds beyond human words. The New American Standard Bible (NASB) translates this as, "He will utter a shout, yes, He will raise a war cry . . . Now like a woman in labor I will groan, I will both gasp and pant." So, the warrior utters a shout and "raises a war cry," while the woman groans, gasps, and pants. Each metaphor deepens the meaning of the other, bringing an almost visceral experience to the reader.

Both are images of courage and strength. While the possibility of danger, pain, and even death is evident in a warrior heading into battle, the laboring mother also faces these same threats. "Childbirth is almost always quite painful, even in the best of situations."[12] Even with today's medical technology, labor is a long, often painful, and dangerous process. Without modern medicine, that danger was increased exponentially, to the point that "because of the mortality rates of women of childbearing age, the life expectancy of women was around 30, while for men it was around 40."[13]

---

11. Dille, *Mixing Metaphors*, 2.
12. Dille, *Mixing Metaphors*, 2.
13. Dille, *Mixing Metaphors*, 29.

However, even in her pain and vulnerability, "the cries and panting of a woman in labor is not a sign of weakness but of strength; a sign of her determination to ensure that her child enters the world alive and healthy."[14] The comparisons continue: the "mother risked death and was the deliverer of new life just as the warrior risked death and was the deliverer of autonomy and peace for the nation."[15] This passage provides metaphors of God as a powerful man of war and as a powerful woman bringing forth life, of God as a Mother/Warrior. Giving birth is profoundly female but in applying this metaphor to God, the image of God is not weakened. This picture adds new and deeper dimensions to the understanding of God in a way no other metaphor could, as Warrior and Mother.

ISAIAH 45:9–11

> Woe to you who strive with your Maker,
> earthen vessels with the potter!
> Does the clay say to the one who fashions it, "What are you making"?
> or "Your work has no handles"?
> Woe to anyone who says to a father, "What are you begetting?"
> or to a woman, "With what are you in labor?"
> Thus says the LORD,
> the Holy One of Israel, and its Maker:
> Will you question me about my children,
> or command me concerning the work of my hands?

The context of this verse is of the Israelites in exile, and the "bone of contention apparently is Cyrus, as well as [God's] whole plan of redemption which centers on Cyrus. . . . Here the implied question is, Why is Cyrus your anointed? The hubris of the clay in questioning the artisan is ludicrous."[16] As Dille explains, it was commonly understood that God formed the child in the womb in the act of creation, connecting God strongly with childbirth. This passage provides us with a parallel. As Dille notes, "The development of the child in the womb is analogous to the work of the artisan in clay."[17] This parallel highlights the absurdity of the situation; God's people

---

14. Claassens, *Mourner, Mother, Midwife*, 26.

15. Brenner and Van Dijk-Hemmes, *On Gendering Texts*, 94, quoted in Claassens, *Mourner, Mother, Midwife*, 50.

16. Dille, *Mixing Metaphors*, 116.

17. Dille, *Mixing Metaphors*, 116.

questioning God's plans is as ridiculous as the artisan's clay questioning the artisan's creation, as ridiculous as questioning a father about begetting his child or questioning a mother about what she is birthing. There is much more to be mined here in contrast between Israel's God and the gods of the surrounding cultures. However, for this chapter, it should be noted that God, interacting with Israel, found an appropriate comparison for herself not only in the artisan and father metaphors, as may be expected, but also in the mother metaphor. Moreover, this metaphor was applied in the leadership context of world governments, further strengthening the appropriateness of mothering metaphors and the role of mothers far outside the realm of complementarian or intensive mothering ideals.

ISAIAH 49:14–15

"But Zion said, 'The LORD has forsaken me, my Lord has forgotten me.' Can a woman forget her nursing child, or show no compassion for the child of her womb? Even these may forget, yet I will not forget you." Isaiah 49:15 reads as if it is a rhetorical question; of course a woman could not forget her nursing child! Even if her mental and emotional state would allow it, which is difficult to imagine in any age, culture, or circumstance, her physical state would not. A mother's body, in the form of over-full breasts, would issue a painful reminder to the mother to feed her child should she ignore this task for too long. This acknowledgment notwithstanding, this passage begins not by *comparing* God's faithful compassion and care with that of a nursing mother but by *contrasting* it. "The stereotype functioning here is the idea of mother-love being the most intense and loyal love there is. The nursing mother is an especially powerful image, combining the absolute dependence of the child on the mother with the mother's own emotional and physical need to nurse."[18] While mothers are generally understood to present the epitome of human love, protection, and care, "Deutero-Isaiah suggests that, although unlikely, it is not unthinkable that a mother would abandon her child."[19] However, although Zion feels abandoned, perhaps experiencing the extreme and unusual desolation of a child abandoned by his mother, "God's love surpasses even the strongest bond between mothers and their children."[20] God as Mother does not forget nor abandon her

18. Dille, *Mixing Metaphors*, 144–45.
19. Dille, *Mixing Metaphors*, 137.
20. Claassens, *Mourner, Mother, Midwife*, 51.

children. The use of the mothering metaphor in this instance adds strength to the understanding of God's love and care. Although not the point of this passage, as this metaphor is applied in the context of the entire Israelite people, it further reminds the reader of the influential role mothers fill and the appropriateness of mothering outside the confining roles often placed on mothers today.

ISAIAH 49:20-21

> The children born in the time of your bereavement
> will yet say in your hearing:
> "The place is too crowded for me;
> make room for me to settle."
> Then you will say in your heart,
> "Who has borne me these?
> I was bereaved and barren,
> exiled and put away—
> so who has reared these?
> I was left all alone—
> where then have these come from?"

In this passage, the metaphor shifts to Zion as mother. "The compassionate and powerful motherhood of God is expressed in contrast to Zion's own shortcomings as the mother of the exiled people."[21] Here, Zion is the city of Jerusalem personified as mother to her inhabitants, or rather, her ex-inhabitants. Zion is "portrayed as a woman and her children, also [signifying] the former and future residents of Jerusalem . . . the exiles in Babylon."[22] In this metaphor, the city of Zion represents a woman bereaved of her children, who are in exile and therefore lost to her. She perceives herself as abandoned by her husband (God), barren and hopeless; she sees no recourse to bearing more children and therefore she has no future. As a result, she is confused; in her bereavement so many children are born that they are crowded, without enough room to settle. "The central issue of this pericope is Zion's childlessness and thereafter her astonishing multitude of children."[23] As the Israelites, the children of Zion, return from exile, "not

---

21. Dille, *Mixing Metaphors*, 129.
22. Dille, *Mixing Metaphors*, 130.
23. Dille, *Mixing Metaphors*, 140.

only does [God] remember Zion, but [God] will reverse [Zion's] own forgetful state and restore her children."[24]

Because it is uniquely maternal, the metaphor in this passage pulls out Zion's vulnerability, desolation, and subsequent renewed hope in a way that another metaphor could not, while still emphasizing the place of honor that the city of Zion would have held in the hearts of the Israelites. The "mother" metaphor is complex and rich, able to incorporate the full spectrum of the mothering experience.

MATTHEW 23:37

"Jerusalem, Jerusalem, the city that kills the prophets and stones those who are sent to it! How often have I desired to gather your children together as a hen gathers her brood under her wings, and you were not willing!" In this verse, the motherhood metaphor shifts again as Jesus expresses his longing in a way that places him in a maternal role. Like the God of the Old Testament, Jesus "wants to shelter and protect the chicks, Jerusalem's children. . . . [This] pictures gathering the young, and the wings belong to a female bird with a 'brood.' The maternal reference in this New Testament passage is explicit."[25] Although the person of Jesus is clearly male and not physically a mother, the metaphor he chose most appropriate to his situation, that best expressed his desire to gather and protect, was a maternal one. Although filled with longing, this is not a picture of an inability to affect change. Jesus is capable of this gathering and protection if only Jerusalem's children were willing. This metaphor reveals a maternal picture of Jesus that, although limited by wayward children, is still fully capable. While the point of this passage is not to raise the perceived value of mother-work or to remove mothering from the confines of today's motherhood expectations, the fact that Jesus chose to express himself using a mothering metaphor accomplishes just that.

GALATIANS 4:12, 19–20

"Friends, I beg you, become as I am, for I also have become as you are. You have done me no wrong. . . . My little children, for whom I am again in the

24. Dille, *Mixing Metaphors*, 143.
25. Bulkeley, *Not Only a Father*, 15.

pain of childbirth until Christ is formed in you, I wish I were present with you now and could change my tone, for I am perplexed about you." In these verses, Paul reaches out to the Galatians, taking the first step. He asks them to become as he is, but this is not a one-sided request. "Paul is calling the Galatians to turn back toward him, because he himself has moved toward them."[26] This request has a specific purpose. As Eastman shares, "In effect, he says to his converts: 'Become as I am now—free from the law. For I also was once as you now want to be—under the law. But through Christ I died to the law that divides Jew and Gentile.'"[27] Paul, who had once lived an exemplary life under the law, now lives free from the law in Christ and in this way, he has become as they are. However, there are apparently teachers among the Galatians, enticing them to live under the law (specifically the law of circumcision). This alarms Paul, who calls them to live as he is, free from the law.

It is in this context that Paul uses a startling metaphor. To connect with the Galatian church, he refers to himself as being in labor. It is important to note that "Galatians 4:19 is not, as commonly understood, an emotional outburst peripheral to the real 'meat' of the letter; it reflects Paul's convictions about the Christocentric character of the gospel."[28] While the supposed "outburst" is certainly attention-grabbing, it is also rich with theological meaning. First, "commentators are fairly unanimous in seeing 4:19 as a reference to Paul's founding of the Galatian congregations. The clue to the material content of Paul's birth pangs is in the word 'again' . . . Paul must repeat something he has done previously."[29]

Even though this congregation, founded by Paul, had been following Christ, now Paul is experiencing "the physical labor, even pain, that accompanies human birth. Paul's claim to be doing something that is manifestly impossible—giving birth (again!)—immediately attracts attention."[30] However, although Paul claims to be in labor with the Galatians, it is not the Galatians who are to be born, but rather, "the object of the labor is Christ who is coming to birth among the Galatians."[31] In the ancient Greco-Roman culture that viewed womanhood and female functions such as labor and

---

26. Eastman, *Recovering Paul's Mother Tongue*, 31.
27. Eastman, *Recovering Paul's Mother Tongue*, 39.
28. Gaventa, *Our Mother Saint Paul*, intro.
29. Eastman, *Recovering Paul's Mother Tongue*, 97–98.
30. Gaventa, *Our Mother Saint Paul*, ch. 2.
31. Gaventa, *Our Mother Saint Paul*, ch. 2.

birth as inferior and shameful, Paul revealed a counter-cultural, subversive viewpoint. The situation addressed in this passage is a complicated one; the laboring mother metaphor is complex enough to express both Paul's concern for the Galatians and the theology he conveys.

1 THESSALONIANS 2:5-8

> As you know and as God is our witness, we never came with words of flattery or with a pretext for greed; nor did we seek praise from mortals, whether from you or from others, though we might have made demands as apostles of Christ. But we were gentle among you, like a nurse tenderly caring for her own children. So deeply do we care for you that we are determined to share with you not only the gospel of God but also our own selves, because you have become very dear to us.

Paul referred to himself and his coworkers in his address to the Thessalonians. There is some discussion on whether he used the descriptive "gentle" as translated here or initially used the word translated as "infant." With solid arguments for both translations, "Paul is striving to express an emotion and lands on a metaphor that gets his point across effectively and dramatically: without the Thessalonians Paul feels as lost as a child bereft of his parents."[32] This ties in nicely with the sentences immediately preceding; Paul denied that he and his coworkers came to the Thessalonians with impure motives or actions. Instead, they came as infants in all innocence and sincerity. McNeel's paraphrase is helpful: "For we never came with flattering words (just as you know), nor with a motive of greed (as God is witness), nor seeking honor from human beings, whether from you or from others (though we could have insisted on our own importance as apostles of Christ), but we were infants in your midst."[33] This usage of the term "infant" further explains how Paul viewed not just himself as an apostle but the role of apostles overall:

> In the past, interpreters have strongly resisted the idea that Paul would use the word "infants" to describe what apostles are like, but Gaventa rightly draws attention to the fact that Paul had an upside-down view of apostles that ran counter to then-prevalent cultural standards of honor, status, and even, at times, masculinity.

32. McNeel, *Paul as Infant*, 40–41.
33. McNeel, *Paul as Infant*, 40–41.

To understand apostles of Christ, Gaventa writes, "one must employ categories that seem outrageous outside the context of Pauline paradox."[34]

This approach clarifies the possible confusion of the metaphor immediately following in which Paul referred to himself as a nurse caring for her children, which would otherwise result in Paul simultaneously being represented as both an infant and a nurse.[35] This "upside-down view" is continued in the metaphor of Paul as a nurse, who would likely have been enslaved, in a culture that already viewed women and their roles as "lesser" in society. "In the first century Greco-Roman world, one could not get much lower on the social scale than a female slave nurse."[36] Paul was not the first biblical male to make this comparison. When Paul referred to himself as a nurse "tenderly caring for her own children," we are reminded of Moses in Numbers 11, as discussed earlier in this chapter. "Both apply the role of nurse to a male; and in both instances it is the male in question who identifies himself with the role. Moses, like Paul, nurtured the people. While Moses insists that he did not assume this role for himself, it is nevertheless the role he continues to play in relation to Israel. In the same way, Paul continues to nurture his congregations."[37]

That Paul chose the role of nurse to express this congregational nurture is significant. A nurse was viewed as not only caring for the physical needs of a child but also teaching and imparting character to this same child, specifically through the act of breastfeeding. "More than simply a reference to the general reality that breastmilk is produced by maternal bodies . . . [the cultural assumption was] that milk communicates 'soul' from a mother/nurse to child. . . . Milk shapes the body, soul (or mind), and spirit of the child drinking it with the result that they resemble their nurse and demonstrate loyalty to her and her blood-kin."[38] The result of the Thessalonians receiving this kind of care from Paul would be their resemblance to him in Christian character and loyalty to him and each other, which is their

---

34. McNeel, *Paul as Infant*, 129. McNeel's quotation of Gaventa comes from Gaventa, *Our Mother Saint Paul*, ch. 1.

35. Paul is capable of mixing metaphors in such way. According to Gaventa's view, the word "infant" would enhance the nurse metaphor with the gentleness attributed to an infant. Gaventa, *Our Mother Saint Paul*, ch. 1.

36. McNeel, *Paul as Infant*, 138.

37. Gaventa, *Our Mother Saint Paul*, ch. 1.

38. Myers, *Blessed Among Women?*, 98.

newly formed Christian community/family. This metaphor deepens when considering that "breastfeeding differs from other forms of giving food . . . in that the nurse or nursing mother gives of her own body for the life of the infant. . . . The metaphor indicates that Paul held nothing back from the Thessalonians but gave of himself for their benefit."[39] This congregation would ideally have responded with loyalty to Paul, but Paul was also deeply invested with and to them.

When considering this role of nurse, "Greco-Roman literature presents an image of the nurse as a woman selflessly devoted to her charges."[40] However, the strength of this relationship heightens when "Paul 'intensifies the tenderness of the image by indicating a woman already known for tenderness in her work, but this time with her own children.'"[41] Here, Paul communicated the shaping of the souls and minds of the Thessalonians through giving himself, not only with the careful and tender affection of a nurse but also as a mother caring for her own nursing child. These metaphors contain many layers; no other metaphors could communicate the depth and intensity of Paul's formational relationship with the Thessalonians. Women and men looking for maternal examples in the Bible have a rich resource in Paul's writings.

JOHN 3:3–8

> Jesus answered him, "Very truly, I tell you, no one can see the kingdom of God without being born from above." Nicodemus said to him, "How can anyone be born after having grown old? Can one enter a second time into the mother's womb and be born?" Jesus answered, "Very truly, I tell you, no one can enter the kingdom of God without being born of water and Spirit. What is born of the flesh is flesh, and what is born of the Spirit is spirit. Do not be astonished that I said to you, 'You must be born from above.' The wind blows where it chooses, and you hear the sound of it, but you do not know where it comes from or where it goes. So it is with everyone who is born of the Spirit."

This passage in which a teacher of the law, Nicodemus, approaches Jesus in the night to question him, results in perhaps one of the most foundational

---

39. McNeel, *Paul as Infant*, 134.
40. McNeel, *Paul as Infant*, 78.
41. Malherbe, *Letters to the Thessalonians*, 147, quoted in McNeel, *Paul as Infant*, 57.

sections of Scripture for the whole of the Christian faith. Jesus's answer, although spoken of the spiritual, is maternal in nature and Nicodemus understands it as such. Nicodemus's follow-up question—"Can one enter a second time into the mother's womb and be born?"—demonstrates that although he wholly misses the spiritual aspect of Jesus's teaching, he does understand the connection between a child being born and the necessity of a mother to birth that child. While Jesus corrects Nicodemus's misunderstanding on the spiritual level, rather than contradicting his understanding of the maternal aspect of birth "from above," Jesus instead builds on it, using water and spirit imagery. Although "the 'water' mentioned in John 3:5 could refer to baptism . . . it is more likely [referring] to the amniotic fluid, the breaking of the waters at birth."[42] There is a distinction between baptism and birth (amniotic fluid). This author contends that baptism, along with the water involved, symbolizes more than death and resurrection. Baptism and baptismal water also symbolize birth, connecting this passage and others that reference being "born again." The understanding that baptism symbolizes birth becomes apparent as the baptismal candidate, after being lowered beneath the water, is "raised to walk in newness of life."[43] Baptism is the outward sign of an internal change; it is the sign of being "born again."

While it is essential to recognize the maternal in this passage and others, care must be taken to remember this is symbolic metaphor rather than a literal understanding, viewing the Spirit of God as a literal female mother. This view results in many of the same issues viewing God as a literal father produces, albeit coming from a different direction, as discussed at the beginning of this chapter. In addition, if we attempt to separate the Trinity into specific sexes and subsequently designate the Spirit as feminine,

> for all practical purposes, we end up with two clear masculine images and an amorphous feminine third. Furthermore, the overarching framework of this approach again remains androcentric, with the male principle still dominant and sovereign. The Spirit even as God remains the "third" person, easily subordinated to the other two since she proceeds from them and is sent by them to mediate their presence and bring to completion what they have initiated.[44]

---

42. Witherington, "Waters of Birth," 155–60, quoted in Massyngberde Ford, *Redeemer Friend and Mother*, 122.

43. Church of the Nazarene, *Manual*, part VIII.

44. Johnson, *She Who Is*, 50.

With this caution in mind, it is still interesting that "though talk of being 'born again' is popular, no thought is given today to the mother that such 'birth' implies."[45] While those who claim the Christian faith commonly recognize themselves as "born of the Spirit," it is far less common to find among those same Christians those who would claim this same Spirit to be maternal. Although this line of thought is often unrecognized, it is not an anomaly; instead, this idea ties much of Scripture together. "The Hebrew Bible's images of God as a woman in labor reach their culmination in the New Testament picture of the Spirit giving new birth through the suffering love of Christ. The image of God as a Mother bringing forth life serves as a unifying strand throughout biblical revelation."[46] Biblical authors are far from presenting birthing and mothering as inferior, nor do they present the women who birth and mother as inferior, as their cultural contexts may have assumed. Biblical authors instead recognized these actions and persons as fitting metaphors for God. This recognition is true to such a degree that the entire Christian faith is built on these birthing, and therefore mothering, metaphors.

1 CORINTHIANS 6:15

"Do you not know that your bodies are members of Christ?" Paul's reference here to the incarnation, death, and resurrection of Jesus helps us realize that "Christians are members of this dead and risen body, and they are such by reason of their own bodies."[47] "Readers often regard this theology of the church as simply a beautiful metaphor. However, we must, shocking though this idea may be, see through to the realism that characterizes the Pauline approach. He is speaking of the real body of Christ, which he looks upon as an extension of the incarnation."[48] This theology includes female bodies as well as male ones. In fact, "metaphors of birthing and nursing and nurture offer an important counterpoint to the lingering perception that Paul's language about 'flesh' and 'spirit' signals a negative attitude toward

---

45. Bulkeley, *Not Only a Father*, 35.
46. Clanton, *In Whose Image?*, 34, quoted in Smith, *Is It Okay*, 140.
47. Gutiérrez, *We Drink*, 68.
48. Gutiérrez, *We Drink*, 69. Although Gutiérrez is speaking in the context of the oppression of systemic poverty, the principle applies just as well to the context of oppression based on gender.

BIBLICAL METAPHORS OF GOD AS MOTHER

the human body."[49] God intends to redeem the entirety of God's children, body and soul. "We are in the presence here of a transformation of the entire human being . . . [emphasizing] the corporeal, material aspect of the human being involved in this process."[50] While the female body has often been viewed with suspicion or animosity, and the whole of womanhood has been viewed this way as well, it is clear that God, who created both female and male in God's image, does not hold that view. Instead, God redeems her children in their entirety.

Labor, birth, breastfeeding, compassion, nurture, formation, shelter, protection: mothering metaphors found in Scripture express spiritual truths in unique ways; no other metaphors suffice. The above passages take "women's reality so abhorred in classical Christian anthropology—the female body and its procreative functions—and [affirm] them as suitable metaphor for the divine."[51] Both the Old and New Testaments apply maternal imagery to God as the first person of the Trinity and the Holy Spirit, and in the New Testament, to Jesus. This maternal imagery begs the question: when we find God in the Bible, what do we find God doing? Often, we find God engaged in the actions of mothering. It is important to note that because "mother" is an appropriate metaphor for God, it is impossible to put the role of "mother" inside patriarchal motherhood restrictions. This is as impossible as it would be to put the role of "father" inside such restrictions. Other biblical figures, such as Moses, Deutero-Isaiah, and Paul, also found in the maternal experience suitable metaphors to apply to themselves and God's people.

Women who grapple with today's unrealistic motherhood ideals are indeed called to Christian ideals instead, including the call to holiness. They are blessed with a rich array of Scriptures containing both female and male imagery as they answer this call.[52] These metaphors and more allow women and men to find themselves in Scripture and Christian thought, and to view themselves as reflections of the image of God in which they are created. Rather than presenting a picture of a weaker God, as some have supposed, these maternal metaphors instead balance out the paternal metaphors so often used; they create a more complete picture of God. Indeed, just as they

49. Gaventa, *Our Mother Saint Paul*, part 2.
50. Gutiérrez, *We Drink*, 67.
51. Johnson, *She Who Is*, 235.
52. All people are called to these Christian ideals, not just those who are mothers. All people are also blessed with this same array of Scriptures, regardless of gender.

did for Maria and Luis, and as they have done for believers throughout faith history, maternal metaphors enrich the Christian community for females and males, without which our community is incomplete.

4

Notable Mothers in Christian History

Two things stood out to Keisha when she thought back on her childhood: one, she grew up in church; and two, she grew up poor. Her experience with the latter had made her determined that her adulthood would be different than her childhood; this became especially pressing once she had children. Keisha ensured that her two daughters would not experience the same struggle to find decent clothes to wear from an inadequate wardrobe, the same taunting over their hairstyles, or lack thereof; they would not be teased because they ate their free lunches at school. They would not be embarrassed, as she had been, to be dropped off by the school bus at the trailer park and then walk to the smallest, dingiest trailer in the lot. Her daughters would not ever experience the shame and stigma that came from being an outsider because of their income bracket; she knew they would have enough of that based on their skin color. Keisha may have started poor, but she had worked hard and now was proud to support an upper-middle-class life for herself, her girls, and occasionally her boyfriend. She had made that happen, and she felt good about it.

Her memories of church brought a different, less straightforward reaction. She thought back to what had been her community; her church had almost been like family. They had called it that, often referring to their "church family." Members habitually called each other "brother" and "sister." They had acted like family too. Sometimes, this meant conflict over some issue, but most often, it told her that this group would be there for her. She remembered her mother baking casseroles when Brother or Sister So-and-So was sick or watching other kids from Sunday school when those kids' parents had to work. The kindness went both directions, as both dinners and offers of help poured in when Grandpa was first in the hospital and then passed away. Keisha smiled fondly as she thought of the strong, sometimes intimidating but generally warm women who made up the core of what might now be known as a "hospitality committee." Back then, they weren't organized by committee; they acted when needed. Keisha reflected with a chuckle that this probably meant a robust gossip/prayer chain, but it worked.

Unfortunately, that old congregation was aging and fading away; many young people had left for school, jobs, or various opportunities. This is precisely what Keisha had done. It had been worth it, and she had proven she could support and raise her daughters well, but she did miss that old church family. Her brow wrinkled as she thought of her attempts to find a new "church family" when she first moved to her current town. Although Keisha was stressed out by the pressures of being a good mother and excelling at work, and although she missed the support she remembered from her childhood, she had not successfully found a new faith community. Every church she visited expected that since she had children, she should be staying home with them, devoting herself to being a wife and mother. This, when she wasn't even a wife! But why would she stay home? She would lose all that she had worked for, and there was no way she was going to go backward financially. She didn't want her daughters to face that kind of life, but that wasn't the kind of life she wanted for herself, either.

She thought of one particular Mother's Day when the sermon was on the ideal mother. The text had been from Prov 31, but the connections the male pastor had drawn from that chapter in the Bible to mothers today hadn't made sense to her. As far as Keisha was concerned, the woman in Prov 31 was an excellent role model for someone like her—that woman not only took care of her family but also went after it in the business world, making sure everything was paid for and taken care of. The woman in Prov 31 wasn't one to sit back and let her husband be in charge of making the money. Instead, she went out and made it herself. So then why, when looking up Prov 31, did the pastor preach on keeping the house tidy, cooking a good dinner, and dressing up—complete with a fresh coat of lipstick—before husbands came home from work? It's not like Keisha couldn't cook, and goodness knows she could bake a casserole with the best of them, but what did that have to do with Prov 31? Wasn't there more to this biblical character, and more character that she revealed?

Further, what if she were the one coming home from work? Should she put lipstick on then? She reflected on the women from the Bible she remembered learning about in Sunday school. It seemed like they also had their interests—didn't they take charge when the situation called for it? In her estimation, the church women she had grown up with fit right in with those women of the Bible. Except for this mysterious "Proverbs 31 woman," who both was and wasn't in the Bible she had right in front of her.

Was the difference that now she was a mother? Shouldn't she work to support her family even more, now that she had children, than when she only had herself to care for? It was baffling. If this was what the church expected of her as a mother and person, why would she ever want to attend church? Although that Mother's Day sermon had been a turning point in her search for a new church family, Keisha still sometimes wondered if something had happened between when the Bible had been written and now, some kind of manipulation to make the Bible say something she didn't understand from a straight reading. Was there some history that had changed what the church expected from her? Who were the Christian mothers in history, anyway? Were they more like the women Keisha read about in the Bible or like that pastor's description of Prov 31—"a submissive wife and mother?"

As Keisha suspects and as discussed in previous chapters, biblical mothers and mothering metaphors fail the standards of today's intensive or complementarian motherhood. Instead, they unveil strong women who overflow the bounds of patriarchal motherhood and metaphors that reveal theological truths while validating the acts and physical realities involved in mothering. The women and metaphors highlighted in these Scripture passages cumulatively direct the believer to prioritize a life of faith, hearing and obeying God's Word, and certainly do not reveal a spirituality mediated by some man. It is important to recognize that mothering is valued in the Bible.[1] However, mothering examples in the Bible reveal a different

---

1. This is the case although mothers themselves were generally viewed as having less value than men and held little or no power in their social settings. The absolute authority the patriarchs held over all family members, the lack of voice demonstrated in the resultant maneuverings of the matriarchs, the mistreatment of Hagar, Bilhah, and Zilpah, and the cultural context Mary was born into all reflect this.

balance than today's mothering standards account for, allowing for a life that prioritizes faith rather than society's expectations. It is clear that many mothers today struggle with this balance, often prioritizing mothering and society's motherhood standards over all else. How did Christian mothers throughout history find this balance, or did they? Which mothers did the church uphold as exemplary, and why? This chapter will highlight the lives of several historical Christian mothers: Perpetua, Monica, Paula, Dhuoda, Julian of Norwich, Jane de Chantal, Susanna Wesley, Sojourner Truth, and Phoebe Palmer. As demonstrated, none of these women fully fit within the bounds of patriarchal motherhood. Instead, these women found their balance as Christian mothers, each employing unique mothering actions. While their mothering actions differed, each of these mothers found their own way to hear God's word and do it.

PERPETUA

Vivia Perpetua lived in Carthage, North Africa, during the years 181–203 CE. The editor of Perpetua's autobiographic narrative (sometimes believed to be Tertullian) described her as "respectably born, liberally educated, a married matron . . . [with] a son an infant at the breast. She herself was about twenty-two years of age."[2] She was also a catechumen, revealing she was a recent convert to Christianity. Perpetua's account of the events surrounding her martyrdom reveals the perspective and attitude of at least one mother of the time, albeit an exemplary one.[3] Much of Perpetua's experience is written in her own words, giving valuable first-hand insight into her imprisonment. She and the others arrested with her were taken into a dungeon and Perpetua reported, "I was very much afraid, because I had never felt such darkness. O terrible day! O the fierce heat of the shock of the soldiery, because of the crowds! I was very unusually distressed by my anxiety for my infant."[4] Perpetua experienced "crowded conditions and rough

---

2. Tertullianus, *Tertullian*, 15.

3. Perpetua's account also includes Felicitas, her servant-companion who birthed a child while imprisoned, awaiting martyrdom herself. Felicitas is also considered a faithful martyr. Her martyrdom is made all the more meaningful because as a servant she lacked the position and voice that Perpetua possessed, yet still remained a powerful witness.

4. Tertullianus, *Tertullian*, 16.

treatment by the soldiers," making the heat "unbearable."[5] However, it was her worry over her baby that "unusually distressed" her.

Soon after, some deacons arranged payment for Perpetua and her companions to be temporarily moved to a better part of the prison where she was allowed her son. She wrote,

> I suckled my child, which was now enfeebled with hunger. In my anxiety for it, I addressed my mother and comforted my brother, and commended to their care my son. . . . I suffered for many days, and I obtained for my infant to remain in the dungeon with me; and forthwith I grew strong and was relieved from distress and anxiety about my infant; and the dungeon became to me as it were a palace, so that I preferred being there to being elsewhere.[6]

Perpetua as a mother is significantly invested in the welfare of her son, even as she is facing persecution, imprisonment, and eventual martyrdom. Her own words communicate that her primary complaint about being in prison was that she was separated from her baby and worried about him, asking her family to care for him. She was so thoroughly invested that the extremity of her stress and worry over her infant's welfare negatively affected her physical well-being. Her situation was only relieved when she could care for her son, allowing her to "regain her strength," albeit in prison. The dungeon that at first terrified her was now, in comparison, "a palace." This concern for her child was not evidence of a mother who would not allow others to care for her child, although Perpetua did demonstrate she was attached to her child. In Perpetua's era, as in most of human history, an infant's only option for nourishment was through breastfeeding. Without this option, Perpetua knew her son would starve. Perpetua herself confirmed this when she shared her father's pleas: "My father came to me . . . worn out with anxiety . . . saying, 'Have pity my daughter . . . have regard to your son, who will not be able to live after you.'"[7] Therefore, this was not a case of others neglecting to provide care; others were not capable of providing care.[8]

Perpetua's account continues with an opportunity for her to renounce Christianity by offering a sacrifice for the emperor, thus saving her own life and therefore also that of her son. Although she was both a mother and a

---

5. Tyson, *Invitation to Christian Spirituality*, 60.
6. Tertullianus, *Tertullian*, 16–17.
7. Tertullianus, *Tertullian*, 18.
8. Perpetua was rich enough to find a wet nurse, but this is not mentioned as an alternative in the text.

daughter, Perpetua's commitment to her Christian faith was primary and outweighed all other roles. This resolve was unusual not only as a mother but also as a daughter who, in that highly patriarchal culture, did not defer to the assumed leadership of her father.[9] Both of these human commitments were presented to her in explicit terms; she could offer the sacrifice, stay with her family and care for her infant, or she could refuse and be martyred. There was no option to refuse to sacrifice and stay with her family. Perpetua described the pivotal moment of her final decision involving her father and son: "Then they came to me, and my father immediately appeared with my boy . . . and said in a supplicating tone, 'Have pity on your babe.' And Hilarianus the procurator . . . said, 'Spare the grey hairs of your father, spare the infancy of your boy, offer sacrifice. . . . And I replied, 'I will not do so.' Hilarianus said, 'Are you a Christian?' And I replied, 'I am a Christian.'"[10] This resulted in her condemnation "to the wild beasts," and she was subsequently returned to the dungeon.

Following this occasion, Perpetua requested that her son, who had previously stayed with her in her prison cell, be returned to her; her father refused. She wrote, "And even as God willed it, the child no long desired the breast, nor did my breast cause me uneasiness, lest I should be tormented by care for my babe and the pain of my breasts at once."[11] That Perpetua was immediately relieved of the physical need to nurse is a miracle similar to physical healing, the key difference being that breastfeeding is not an ailment.[12] No less miraculous is an infant who instantly neither needs nor wants to breastfeed. While a male author might overlook this significance, Perpetua attributed this miraculous experience to God. Further, "The addition of such a detail suggests that Perpetua wanted the reader to know that God approved of this mother-child detachment."[13]

When the day of her martyrdom arrived, Perpetua was not the only young mother taken to the arena. Felicitas was pregnant when she was arrested along with the others. She was concerned that she would not be allowed to be martyred with her companions because of her pregnancy

---

9. Perpetua's husband is absent from her account.
10. Tertullianus, *Tertullian*, 18–19.
11. Tertullianus, *Tertullian*, 19.
12. Breastfeeding itself is not an ailment, however, a sudden stop to breastfeeding, rather than a gradual weaning process, leads to painful physical ailments. Perpetua would not have had access to modern medicine that today is capable of safely facilitating this shortened physical transition.
13. Marga, *In the Image*, 34.

and instead be executed with criminal strangers later. As the result of the prayers of the group, Felicitas, at eight months, gave birth to a girl, "which a certain sister brought up as her daughter."[14] In a culture that abandoned unwanted infants, it is notable that the church community assumed care for this female, premature baby. On the day of their martyrdom Felicitas was "rejoicing that she had safely brought forth, so that she might fight with the wild beasts; from the blood and from the midwife to the gladiator, to wash after childbirth with a second baptism."[15] Perpetua, Felicitas, and the other Christians being martyred, faced their deaths, "joyous and of brilliant countenances . . . [and] Perpetua sang psalms."[16]

Perpetua had great concern for her child and cared for his well-being, as demonstrated by her discussions with her family concerning his care, her desire to breastfeed, and her requests to keep her baby with her. However, her primary commitment was as a follower of Christ; she joyfully proved this with her life. Perpetua and Felicitas took countercultural actions in their defiance of the Roman government, their relinquishment of their infants, and Perpetua's resistance to her father's pleading. Both women are considered exemplary by the church. Although these actions were outside the accepted norms for "womanly behavior" of the day, at times they have been interpreted otherwise. For example, "Augustine's theology of subordination was so strong that he manipulated a renowned martyrdom account to suit his own purposes. Perpetua personifies the dutiful daughter and devoted mother in Augustine's text. Augustine could not portray Perpetua as anything but the 'good' (i.e., submissive and obedient) Christian woman."[17]

---

14. Tertullianus, *Tertullian*, 25.
15. Tertullianus, *Tertullian*, 26.
16. Tertullianus, *Tertullian*, 26.

17. Leclerc, *Singleness of Heart*, 47. Also, see Leclerc, *Discovering Christian Holiness*. Perpetua's pagan father tries, unsuccessfully, to convince her to deny her faith so that she can raise her child as she ought. She refused his pleas, and subsequently he had the child taken from her. How does Perpetua have such resolve, one so strong that it caused her to deny her responsibilities as parent and to defy her place as daughter? She shows forth a singleness of heart that allowed her to devote herself entirely to God's will. The original text itself offers explicit approval for Perpetua's release from the cares and anxieties of motherhood, attributing such to divine intervention. While it could be argued that the more prevalent perception of female martyrs and virgins as "virile" and "manly" is androcentric, such a perception at least opens the door to an appropriation of a certain level of autonomy by the women undertaking lives of ascetic renunciation. This theme will continue throughout the patristic period. Women like Perpetua are models of a single-hearted holiness.

Augustine's portrayal foreshadows today's complementarian theology. He manages this, however, in opposition to the martyr's own written perspective, which "offers explicit approval for Perpetua's release from the cares and anxieties of motherhood, attributing such to divine intervention."[18]

Augustine's "complementarian" interpretation notwithstanding, it is difficult to draw comparisons from the account of the Christian mothers Perpetua and Felicitas to Christian mothers today. Perpetua and Felicitas did not conform to the expectations placed on them in their time, having "abandoned their newborns for the beasts' arena,"[19] and they likewise would not live up to the expectations they would hypothetically face as mothers today. "Their actions, their devotion to Christ, and their relinquishment of the role of mother have been celebrated in the Christian tradition since the second century."[20] They are celebrated still.

MONICA

Monica was born into a Christian family in the North African town of Tagaste in about the year 332 CE. As a child, Monica was known for her prayers.[21] Knowing this background of prayer, it may be surprising to learn that she had a brush with alcoholism as a girl. It was her duty each day to go down to the cellar and retrieve the wine for the family's meal. She began to sip the wine, and over time, her habit grew. Eventually, she was drinking entire cupfuls. On one of these occasions, she argued with a household servant; the argument became heated. In anger the servant called Monica a derogatory name; Augustine referred to it as "the most bitterly insulting language."[22] This insult has been translated as "wine-swiller,"[23] "little lush,"[24] "a bibber of pure wine, a drunkard—or as we now say, an alcoholic."[25] Monica recognized the truth in this insult and was convicted; she immediately changed her ways.

---

18. Tertullianus, *Tertullian*, 26.
19. Marga, *In the Image*, 12.
20. Marga, *In the Image*, 12–13.
21. Cristiani, *Story of Monica*, 25.
22. Augustine, *Works of Saint Augustine*, 9:18.
23. Augustine, *Works of Saint Augustine*, 9:18.
24. Clark, *Monica*, 24.
25. Cristiani, *Story of Monica*, 23.

When she was old enough, her family arranged her marriage to a local man named Patricius, who according to custom would have been many years her senior. Patricius, who was not a Christian, held an official civil position in their community; he also possessed a violent temper and was known to cheat on his wife. In a context where straying husbands and spousal abuse were accepted, Monica was praised for pacifying her husband and advising other young wives to do the same. Her success in calming Patricius was evidenced in her lack of visible bruises resulting from abuse, while other wives commonly displayed them.[26] Although these accounts reveal general acceptance of the appalling treatment of women in that time and context, Augustine did not necessarily view Monica "as allowing herself to be walked upon, but rather as having the self-control to choose her moment. She could be trusted to make her own case when she was met with unjust criticism, but she was cautious about the timing."[27] This patient nature also won over her adversarial mother-in-law[28] and was enough of a witness that her husband became a Christian about a year before his death.[29]

Patricius and Monica had three children: two boys (Augustine and Navigius) and a girl (possibly named Perpetua).[30] Although Patricius did not convert to Christianity until late in life, Monica was influential in raising their children as Christians, as both Navigius and Perpetua were Christians the entirety of their lives. Only Augustine left the faith for a time, beginning in his teen years, greatly distressing his mother. We know that he was raised in faith, not only by the examples of his siblings but also because he became deathly ill as a child. Augustine himself requested baptism, which was not commonly given at such a young age. He shared of his mother, "She . . . was very anxious, because in her pure heart, through her faith in you and with a love still more tender, she was bringing my eternal salvation to birth. She would have hastened to ensure that I was initiated into the saving sacraments and washed clean by confessing you, Lord Jesus, for the forgiveness of my sins."[31] However, Augustine recovered from his illness before being baptized, and the sacrament was delayed.

---

26. Augustine, *Works of Saint Augustine*, 9:19.
27. Leyser and Smith, *Motherhood, Religion, and Society*, 11.
28. Augustine, *Works of Saint Augustine*, 9:20.
29. Augustine, *Works of Saint Augustine*, 9:22.
30. Cristiani, *Story of Monica*, 35–36.
31. Augustine, *Works of Saint Augustine*, 9:17.

By his teen years, Augustine had shown himself to excel in his studies; during these years Augustine fell away from his faith, and Monica began tearfully praying for his return to Christianity. While away in Carthage for his schooling, Augustine began a relationship with a mistress, who he did not marry but with whom he eventually had a son. He also joined a religious group called the Manicheans. When he returned home spouting Manichean philosophies, Monica decided there was no place for those ideas in her house. She refused to let Augustine stay with her. Her husband had passed away by then. However, she had a dream that assured her of Augustine's eventual conversion and relented.[32] It was also during this time that she visited an unnamed bishop and begged him to convince her son to return to Christianity. She was so persistent in her request that "a little vexed, he answered, 'Go away now; but hold on to this: it is inconceivable that he should perish, a son of tears like yours.' In her conversations with [Augustine] she often recalled that she had taken these words to be an oracle from heaven."[33]

As an adult, Augustine embarked upon a successful teaching career, which eventually resulted in a position in Rome. Monica was opposed to his leaving for Rome without her. Although it would be expected that at this point Augustine, as an adult man, could assume his mother's deference to his decision, Augustine recorded that instead Monica "bitterly bewailed my departure and followed me. . . . She held on to me with all her strength, attempting either to take me back home with her or to come with me."[34] She is so insistent on these points that Augustine resorted to trickery, deceiving his mother in order to sail for Rome, leaving her behind "praying and weeping."[35]

Augustine only taught in Rome for a short time before moving to accept another teaching position in Milan. It was here that Monica joined him, taking the unusual steps as a woman to travel overseas alone. In addition to traveling unaccompanied, her voyage was notable as she was the one, rather than the professional sailors, to assure both passengers and crew of their safe journey. She was confident of their safe arrival because of her previous dream, which she understood as God's promise that she would

---

32. Augustine, *Works of Saint Augustine*, 9:19.
33. Augustine, *Works of Saint Augustine*, 9:21.
34. Augustine, *Works of Saint Augustine*, 5:15.
35. Augustine, *Works of Saint Augustine*, 5:15.

see Augustine come to faith.[36] While in Milan, some other perspectives of Monica emerged when she revised her long-held tradition of honoring the dead on the recommendation of Bishop Ambrose.[37] Monica was also among the faithful Christian supporters during the persecution of a church there.[38] Monica was involved in her church and community. However, she continued to be involved in her son's life. Part of this involvement included arranging a marriage for her son,[39] although ultimately Augustine chose to remain single for religious reasons.[40]

After seventeen years of his mother's prayers and tears, Augustine returned to the Christian faith and immediately shared the news with Monica.[41] Soon after Augustine's conversion, Monica, her grandson Adeodatus, Augustine, and a handful of Augustine's friends retreated for six months. They spent time in prayer and study and discussed Scripture and philosophy. Although it was unusual for a woman, Monica participated in these activities. Augustine "presents her to us as a woman of sound judgment, quick perception, and penetrating insights."[42] Following this retreat, Augustine was baptized, and then he and Monica set out for their hometown of Tagaste. During their journey, they stopped in Ostia, where they shared a mystical experience. Looking out their window and deep in discussion, they yearned for God's wisdom. Together,

> [they] step by step traversed all bodily creatures and heaven itself, whence sun and moon and stars shed their light upon the earth. Higher still we mounted by inward thought and wondering discourse on your works, and we arrived at the summit of our own minds; and this too we transcended, to touch that land of never-failing plenty. . . . And as we talked and panted for it, we just touched the edge of it by the utmost leap of our hearts; then, sighing and unsatisfied, we left the first-fruits of our spirit captive

---

36. Augustine, *Works of Saint Augustine*, 6:1.

37. Augustine, *Works of Saint Augustine*, 6:2.

38. The empress demanded the church be turned over to the Arian sect, but the bishop, Ambrose, resisted. Augustine, *Works of Saint Augustine*, 9:15.

39. Augustine, *Works of Saint Augustine*, 6:23.

40. This was after Augustine said goodbye to his long-time mistress and mother of his son, and after taking, then dismissing, another woman as mistress following her departure. Augustine, *Works of Saint Augustine*, 6:15, 25.

41. Augustine, *Works of Saint Augustine*, 8:29, 30.

42. Cristiani, *Story of Monica*, 152.

there, and returned to the noise of articulate speech, where a word has beginning and end.[43]

Not long after this experience, Monica passed away, content that her life on earth was complete.[44]

Monica is another early example of Christian mothering. However, the only information remaining of her originated from her son's writings and could therefore be anticipated to relate only to her life as a mother. Instead, this information includes accounts that portray her as a complete person, albeit from her son's perspective. That this son was the same author that reimagined Perpetua as "submissive and obedient" indicates he may have given Monica the same treatment. However, she still appears as a woman with her own personality, inclinations, and struggles, demonstrated in her brush with alcoholism as a girl. That she overcame this struggle, shows self-control and strength of character. Her life of early prayer must have played into this victory as her continued prayer played into her son's eventual salvation. As a wife, Monica was saddled with the burdens of infidelity and abuse, common to marriages of the era. While her situation reveals the awful conditions women of her time faced, it also reveals a woman with the strength and wisdom to navigate difficult circumstances. In this scenario, she could be considered the model complementarian wife, demonstrating the abuses possible when this philosophy is taken too far. Monica also counseled other women who faced similar forms of mistreatment.

In this challenging setting, Monica raised three children as Christians, pursuing baptism for Augustine when it looked like his young life was close to an end. When Augustine fell away from the Christian faith, she remained strong enough in her convictions to refuse him a place in her home. This refusal was reversed not because she released her convictions but rather because of a divinely inspired dream. Monica's persistence is revealed in her conversations with the unnamed bishop, her attempts to prevent Augustine's travels, her subsequent travels, and her continued tearful prayers for Augustine's salvation. That she was flexible enough to change her practices and grow in faith was evidenced as she followed Bishop Ambrose's direction. That she was firmly committed to her faith was demonstrated as she stood with her persecuted church, supporting her community of faith at her personal risk. Once Augustine did convert to Christianity, Monica demonstrated her intelligence and wisdom as she spent time in prayer and

---

43. Augustine, *Works of Saint Augustine*, 9:24.
44. Augustine, *Works of Saint Augustine*, 9:28.

philosophical discussion with Augustine and his companions, impressing Augustine with her insights. Her spiritual acuity is revealed during their shared mystical experience as they together sought God's wisdom. As a widowed matron, Monica had freedoms she may not have otherwise had. However, she still does not fit the description of submissive and obedient, even as she is filtered through Augustine's perspectives to today's reader. She is depicted as a woman who prioritized mothering well into her children's adult years. She is also depicted as a woman who prioritized faith and was content to pass on once her beloved son had also come to faith. "Although in later studies of Monica, she is often portrayed as being overly attached to her son, rather than being misremembered as an over-involved, hand-wringing mother, Monica deserves to be remembered as a highly successful Christian mother."[45]

As a woman eventually recognized as a saint, Monica fits the bill as someone upheld as exemplary by the church. Unlike Perpetua and Felicitas, Monica was not martyred, leaving behind infant sons. Unlike some of the mothers discussed below, Monica appears to have fully embraced motherhood and mothering. Today's intensive mothering would have contemporary mothers believe there is one way to mother and one way to mother as a Christian; anyone who falls outside of those norms is perceived to fail as a "good" mother. Complementarian mothering only exaggerates and solidifies this perspective, adding layers of religious expectations and the requirement for women to act as submissive wives. Perpetua and Monica, in their differing circumstances, made vastly different choices that resulted in different mothering actions. For these women, there was not "one way" to mother. As with the mothers of the Bible, their lives overflow the bounds of patriarchal motherhood. Whether or not they may have measured up to today's motherhood standards as "good" mothers, they are revealed as women who were exemplary Christians.

PAULA

A very different picture of motherhood arises when we consider Paula, a younger contemporary of Monica's. Paula was born into a prominent Roman family in 347 CE and married "Toxotius in whose veins ran the noble blood of Æneas and the Julii."[46] She had five children. The first four were

---

45. Marga, *In the Image*, 118.
46. Jerome, *Complete Works*, letter 108, para. 4.

girls: Blesilla, Pammachius, Eustochium, and Rufina.[47] "After that, Paula would have stopped bearing children because she would no longer perform the office of marriage. But Paula obeyed the will of her husband, who desired to have a male heir."[48] Paula thus far acted as a woman who followed the cultural script prescribed to her by marrying well, having children, and deferring to her husband's wishes. However, "Paula's story tells of how she set sail for Jerusalem—after the death of her husband—on a pilgrimage, leaving three of her children alone, crying on the shore."[49] Tracy confirms, "Paula's legend is one of contemplation, highlighted by her voluntary separation from her children and her severe lifestyle. She is the picture of marital obedience and motherly love until she forsakes her children to journey to the Holy Land."[50]

The scene of her departure was a dramatic one. "Only one daughter was to accompany her, the ten-year-old Julia Eustochium, who had already vowed to live as a Christian virgin. Paula was leaving behind her older teenage daughter Rufina and her tiny son Toxotius. She would not perform the expected duties of an upper-class Roman mother at Rufina's upcoming wedding."[51] Jerome wrote that as she went to the port to leave, she was accompanied "by her brother, her kinsfolk and above all her own children eager by their demonstrations of affection to overcome their loving mother."[52] It is clear that her children, especially, did not want their mother to leave and hoped to change her mind. Once her ship set sail, "on the shore the little Toxotius stretched forth his hands in entreaty, while Rufina . . . with silent sobs besought her mother to wait. . . . But still Paula's eyes were dry as she turned them heavenwards; and she overcame her love for her children by her love for God. She knew herself no more as a mother, that she might approve herself a handmaid of Christ."[53] Although the text confirms that Paula no longer considered herself a mother and even speaks of her stoic resolve, Marga states, "Their emotional goodbye makes it clear that Paula had strong and loving maternal bonds with her children that were typical

---

47. Jerome, *Complete Works*, letter 108, para. 4.
48. Jerome, *Complete Works*, letter 22, para. 8.
49. Barr, *Making of Biblical Womanhood*, 79.
50. Tracy, *Women*, 45.
51. Marga, *In the Image*, 22.
52. Jerome, *Complete Works*, letter 108, para. 6.
53. Jerome, *Complete Works*, letter 108, para. 6.

of Roman motherhood."[54] That this was a struggle for her was further evidenced by Jerome who wrote, "No mother, it must be confessed, ever loved her children so dearly,"[55] and further, "her heart was rent within her, and she wrestled with her grief, as though she were being forcibly separated from parts of herself. The greatness of the affection she had to overcome made all admire her victory the more."[56]

Although Paula's actions in leaving behind her children would be surprising and possibly shocking in today's culture, they were celebrated in Paula's. Jerome considered Paula's leaving of her dearly loved children to be an admirable victory. In an era that denigrated womanhood and considered women "who bore children . . . as making poor choices about their bodies, dedicating them primarily to earthly things like sex and procreation rather than to God,"[57] Paula was considered to be rising above her earthly, sinful nature. "Paula's relinquishment of her role as mother to her children indicated to theologians like Jerome that she was heading into the process of shedding the attributes of her femaleness that trapped her in her maternal flesh and prevented her from salvation."[58] Leclerc and others suggest that such "singleness of heart" that had radical conclusions and practical consequences was the only means of empowerment for Christian women in the fourth and fifth centuries.[59]

Paula subsequently founded a monastery for women in cooperation with Jerome's monastery founded for men.[60] She also worked alongside Jerome in translating the Bible from Hebrew and Greek into Latin. Although much is made of Paula leaving her children, author Amy E. Marga includes Paula in the following statement when she writes,

> Clearly, they were agents in their own decisions. Each woman seems to have kept in touch with her children, and each one acquired high status and power within the Christian community. These wealthy mothers were surely committed to their families. . . . [They] brought their children into the new communities that they had founded at a later date; neither one ever stopped trying to

---

54. Marga, *In the Image*, 22.
55. Jerome, *Complete Works*, letter 108, para. 6.
56. Jerome, *Complete Works*, letter 108, para. 6.
57. Marga, *In the Image*, 27.
58. Marga, *In the Image*, 30.
59. For a full discussion on this topic, see Leclerc, *Singleness of Heart*, 25–59.
60. Jerome, *Complete Works*, letter 108, para. 20.

> influence the lives of their children, even from afar. It could be that wealthy mothers such as . . . Paula left their children and the rigid conventions of Roman motherhood because they wanted to.[61]

While many of today's readers may find her actions both noble (translating the Bible, founding a monastery) and shocking (leaving her crying children behind), she is remembered admirably for her dedication to God, understanding that "her courage coveted the love of her children as the greatest of its kind, yet she left them all for the love of God."[62] Paula is an example of a mother the church considered exemplary who would not be considered a "good" mother by today's standards, her long-distance communication notwithstanding.

Although Paula was historically celebrated by the church precisely because, as a loving mother, she gave up her children for service to God, in today's culture, that would be unacceptable by most, if not all conservative Christians. In an article discussing the occurrence in pop culture of the "mother's ultimate sin," which is identified as "abandoning her children," Amanda Hess explains, "In each case, her children are not abandoned outright; they are left in the care of fathers and other relatives. When a man leaves in this way, he is unexceptional. When a woman does it, she becomes a monster, or perhaps an antiheroine riding out a dark maternal fantasy."[63] Hess expounds,

> there are so many ways to do motherhood wrong, or so a mother is told. She can be overbearing or remote. She can smother or neglect. She can mother in such a specifically bad way that she is assigned a bad-mom archetype: stage mother, refrigerator mother, "cool mom." She can hover like a helicopter mom or bully like a bulldozer mom. But the thing she cannot do—the thing that is so taboo it rivals actually murdering her offspring—is leave.[64]

Hess references works of fiction in this article and discusses more sympathetic portrayals of women who leave their children with others for personal reasons. However, she has summed up the prevailing attitude of today's culture: that above all else, mothers must remain physically present with their children.

---

61. Marga, *In the Image*, 38.
62. Tracy, *Women*, 47.
63. Hess, "Mommy Is Going Away."
64. Hess, "Mommy Is Going Away."

Again, as with Perpetua, it may be tempting to argue that Paula left her children behind in their best interest, as she was setting a Christian example for them to follow. However, it is clear that Jerome, and by extension the church, considered Paula exemplary precisely because she did not put her children first. She did not allow herself to be caught up in the care of children considered to be "narcissists who distracted mothers from true devotion to God."[65] Clearly, this understanding of children and view of motherhood has changed dramatically since the time of Paula and Jerome. Just as clearly, although venerated as a saint, the life of Paula does not line up with today's motherhood expectations. Just as with Perpetua and Monica, Paula made different choices that resulted in different mothering actions. These women are celebrated as devoted women, not in terms of their maternal role. If their actions seem extreme, at least one lesson is to see them as examples of people who are empowered and draw their value from Christ instead of from the opinions of others. For Paula, there was no "one way" to mother; this was not her ultimate priority. Instead, there was one way for her to "hear the word of God and do it" (Luke 8:21), which was to leave her children behind in entire devotion to God.

DHUODA

Dhuoda was married to Bernard of Septimania, an official at the court of Louis the Pious.[66] Like Perpetua, Dhuoda left us a first-hand perspective of her world, unique because she wrote it personally. Unlike Perpetua, she was not martyred but separated from her sons as they grew up. "In the highly masculinized, unstable culture of the Frankish kingdoms, Dhuoda was forced to give up William and his baby brother into the company of Charles the Bald because of her husband's politics."[67] While her husband and sons were away, it was necessary for Dhuoda to stay behind and assume responsibility for their family property.[68] Her words come to us in the form of a manual written (c. 841–843 CE) for her then fifteen-year-old son William.[69] "Her intention was . . . to ensure [William's] moral and spiritual welfare. 'You will find in my book a mirror,' she told him, 'in which you

---

65. Marga, *In the Image*, 12.
66. Gies and Gies, *Marriage and the Family*, 77.
67. Marga, *In the Image*, 118.
68. Marga, *In the Image*, 119.
69. Gies and Gies, *Marriage and the Family*, 75.

can contemplate the salvation of your soul."[70] "Beyond its uniqueness as an early medieval book of advice written not only by a layperson but by a woman, the enduring value of *Dhuoda's Manual* is the insight it gives into three aspects of the family: feelings within the family circle, authority in the family, and the family consciousness of the ninth-century European aristocracy."[71] Although separated from her sons and unable to mother in a more conventional manner, Dhuoda still did what she could to influence her children. "Dhuoda expressed what seems to be an almost-universal sentiment among mothers: the desire that their child fit into society and be a productive citizen. She wanted William to be pleasing to God and to be 'useful to man.' . . . On a light-hearted note, Dhuoda, like any good mother of a teenager, suggested that maybe William's friends could read her Handbook too."[72]

Dhuoda writes of "religious fundamentals," social and moral conduct based on those religious fundamentals, and then "returns to spiritual matters, to consider how trials and tribulations can be met."[73] She does not solely rely on the views of family and aristocracy but instead builds on Scripture, established theologians (notably Monica's Augustine) and her own insights. "Dhuoda's use of Augustine is remarkable and has been duly remarked on by commentators. . . . Dhuoda's use of the Psalms is much more extensive, evenly distributed throughout the Handbook, and suggestive of deep and independent reflection."[74] This demonstrates that Dhuoda not only thought these points were vital for William to remember as he grew into adulthood, but she also attained knowledge of these points sometime prior to writing her letter. Dhuoda revealed herself as an intelligent, thoughtful theologian exercising the managerial skills required to oversee family properties and mothering from a distance.

Dhuoda also reminded her son William that he might have children in the future. He would then want children who were "modest, peaceful, and obedient," and at that point, he would be glad to have been such a son himself. Further, "he must never forget that to his father he owes his situation in the world."[75] In fact, "Dhuoda spent almost an entire chapter (book

---

70. Gies and Gies, *Marriage and the Family*, 79.
71. Gies and Gies, *Marriage and the Family*, 80.
72. Gies and Gies, *Marriage and the Family*, 129.
73. Leyser and Smith, *Motherhood, Religion, and Society*, 42–43.
74. Leyser and Smith, *Motherhood, Religion, and Society*, 47.
75. Gies and Gies, *Marriage and the Family*, 81–82.

3) explaining how William must revere his father, Bernard. Clearly, she was working with an image of God who is directly related to earthly fathers and patrilineal authority. Obedience to earthly fathers would bring divine reward, and 'fatherly power' was the supreme power on earth."[76]

In Dhuoda, we find a mother who understood the patriarchal society she inhabited and her place in it. Although she was left to manage family holdings, giving her a certain amount of power as a woman of social and material standing, she still deferred to patrilineal authority and conferred this understanding on her children. She was also a mother who prioritized Christian instruction to her son, indicating her view of the importance of living out the Christian faith in the various settings he would face. In this endeavor,

> Dhuoda minimized her authority and intelligence as a woman even though she was probably one of the very few women in her time who were highly educated. . . . The educated references that she made to the Latin Vulgate translation of Scripture and to church Fathers such as Augustine and Gregory the Great belies her self-minimization. Her *Handbook* displays a highly educated, literate woman. In other words, while Dhuoda rejected any pretense of general female intelligence, she used her privilege as the *mother* to William. The *Handbook* reveals Dhuoda exercising her maternal authority by taking up the pen.[77]

In many ways, Dhuoda displayed characteristics and actions of the ideal complementarian mother. She was invested in her children, prioritized Christian instruction, deferred to male headship, and prioritized her role as mother. These characteristics were in place even as she was highly educated and acted as the overseer of her family's land. And yet it required a certain amount of skill, intelligence, and power for her to divest herself of the same. She occupied the space of a strong and independent woman, even as her rhetoric conforms to the ninth-century ideology and practices. She was separated from her children not by choice, as was the case with Paula, but due to circumstances beyond her control. As with many of the mothers of the Bible, in her context the traditional motherhood ideal was not flexible enough to incorporate the variety of circumstances mothers face.

---

76. Marga, *In the Image*, 122.
77. Marga, *In the Image*, 123.

JULIAN OF NORWICH

Julian of Norwich differs from the women discussed in this chapter because we do not know much about her life or if she ever had children. "Because Julian's theology is pervaded by such intimate knowledge of the mother-child bond and knowledge of how the female body works, scholars speculate that she herself likely had been a mother . . . [and] it is likely [her children] succumbed to the bubonic plague."[78] Julian is included here because she provides a unique view of motherhood—that of the motherhood of God.

Julian was born in 1343 CE and suffered a life-threatening illness at the age of thirty. While looking at a crucifix during this illness, she experienced fifteen visions, with a sixteenth vision the following day. These visions resulted in her first manuscript, also known as her "short text." She prayed and meditated on these visions for the following twenty years before writing what is known as her "long text."

"In her visions, Julian saw the blood trickling down from Christ's head under the crown of thorns. . . . Julian made a point to describe Christ's blood as abundant and fresh . . . [suggesting] she saw it as a source of life and joy, similar to the way that the blood that accompanies birth and female fertility is fresh and part of the life-giving process."[79] This indicates that "God does not just tolerate the filth of the maternal body, God *is* the maternal body shedding life-giving uterine blood out of love and the promise of life."[80] In her texts, Julian explained that God's motherhood is demonstrated in creation as children are born, as people are reborn as Christians, and "with all the sweet protection of love which endlessly follows."[81] These mothering actions are described as "the foundation of our nature's creation . . . His taking of our nature, where the motherhood of grace begins . . . [and] the motherhood at work."[82]

Not only is God described as mother, so also is God's son. "And so Jesus is our true Mother in nature by our first creation, and He is our true Mother in grace by His taking our created nature. All the lovely works and all the sweet loving offices of beloved motherhood are appropriated

---

78. Marga, *In the Image*, 55.
79. Marga, *In the Image*, 55–56.
80. Marga, *In the Image*, 56 (emphasis in original).
81. Julian, *Julian of Norwich*, 295.
82. Julian, *Julian of Norwich*, 297.

to the second person."[83] While we do not know with certainty if Julian was a mother herself or what her approach to human motherhood may have been, "for Julian, Christ is the archetypal mother, our true mother from whom all motherhood derives. . . . She never speaks of Christ's being *like* a mother. On the contrary, mothers are like Christ."[84] Julian developed the imagery of Christ our mother in several ways. One of these was to compare mothers who nourish their children with their bodies to Christ nourishing "her" children with "her" own body in the Eucharist. She also spoke of him helping his children grow by teaching and preaching to them, by seeing the needs of his children, by allowing them to be chastised, and through it all, loving his children without end. "The image of Christ as mother is not simply an interesting curiosity within her theology; rather, the motherhood imagery represents the very heart of Julian's mature theology."[85]

Julian wrote of the first person of the Trinity as mother and Christ as mother. She also extended this motherhood imagery to all of the Trinity. "And therefore it is our part to love God in whom we have our being, reverently thanking and praising Him for our creation, mightily praying to our Mother for mercy and pity, and to our Lord the Holy Spirit for help and grace."[86] In fact, "maternal love inflects the work of the whole Trinity. Mother Christ desired humanity and the Father and the Spirit joined in the work to bring this desire to fruition."[87]

While we know Julian dedicated much of her life to Christian service as an anchoress, we do not have enough history to know if her prior life included motherhood.[88] However, she reveals in her writings the maternal love and actions of God. Julian's perspective of God as mother scrambles today's motherhood ideals. Further, the ideals of complementarian mothering, specifically the hierarchical ideals of the submissive wife and mother, fall apart when it is God who is our mother.

83. Julian, *Julian of Norwich*, 296.
84. Palliser, *Christ, Our Mother*, 114 (emphasis in original).
85. Palliser, *Christ, Our Mother*, 110.
86. Julian, *Julian of Norwich*, 296.
87. Farley, *Thirst of God*, 130.
88. While we do not know if Julian was a mother, we do know Margery Kempe, a contemporary of Julian's, was the mother of fourteen children. She birthed her children prior to arranging with her husband to live a celibate life. Kempe visited Julian seeking spiritual direction and shared of their time together, "The anchoress and I had a great deal of holy conversation as we talked about the love of our Lord Jesus Christ during the many days we were together." Kempe, *Book of Margery Kempe*, 49.

JANE DE CHANTAL

Jane was the second child of three born to Benigne Fremyot and Marguerite de Berbeseey in 1572 CE. She was "educated at home by tutors and cared for by an aunt and nurse," also benefitting from her "father's broad humanist views on history, morality, and the law."[89] She lived in a turbulent era and the results of the Reformation reached Jane, who was a faithful Catholic. As a young woman, she turned down a potential suitor, accurately believing him to be a Protestant.[90] She eventually married Baron Christophe Rabutin de Chantal. As a young baroness, she became "responsible for the management of the estate, household and lands. . . . [She also] took it upon herself to assist the poor of the neighborhood."[91] Jane and Christophe had four children who survived infancy, one boy and three girls.[92]

While Jane was still recovering from the birth of her youngest child, Christophe died in a hunting accident. At twenty-eight years old, Jane was now a mother of four and a widow. Months of intense mourning followed Christophe's death. However, "she was drawn to the idea that she should now give herself completely to God rather than follow the path of remarriage."[93] For seven and a half years, responsibilities prevented her from taking either path. Instead, she had an obligation to care for her aging father-in-law and the children he had with his housekeeper, alongside her own four children.[94] However, she connected with Francis de Sales during this time; he became her spiritual director and life-long friend. Francis designed for her a new rule of life, including that "Monica, the patron saint of widows, was to be her novice-mistress and the Virgin Mary, her abbess."[95]

Eventually, Francis de Sales and Jane de Chantal decided to form a religious community for women that would require annual vows (rather than permanent ones), inner mortification (rather than outward austerity), and a simplified office (rather than the formal monastic divine office). In addition, this community would "not have full enclosure and separation from the outside world. Women like Jane, after all, might be called away

---

89. Wright, *Francis de Sales*, 41.
90. Wright, *Francis de Sales*, 19.
91. Wright, *Francis de Sales*, 24.
92. Wright, *Francis de Sales*, 25.
93. Wright, *Francis de Sales*, 33–34.
94. Wright, *Francis de Sales*, 36.
95. Wright, *Francis de Sales*, 46.

to attend family business."⁹⁶ In light of family responsibilities, this community was not established immediately. First, Jane made arrangements for her children. She arranged for her oldest daughter to marry one of Francis's younger brothers. As her daughter was only eleven years old at the time of her marriage,⁹⁷ Jane moved nearby to assist her in running her new household. Jane also arranged schooling for her son and decided to take her two younger daughters to live with her in the newly established community.

Once Jane's children were planned for, the new religious community was ready to be established, and Jane was ready to leave. However, a situation with Jane's son highlighted both Jane's motherhood and religious commitment.

> The adolescent boy launched a passionate appeal for her to stay. His dramatic words ... caught his mother by surprise ... [and] tears welled up in Jane's eyes and when she stepped toward the open street-side door [he] flung himself down across the threshold. ... Jane had no choice but to choke back a sob and step over him. Loudly criticized by two rigidly pious onlookers for her lack of spiritual detachment ... she replied simply that after all, she *was* a mother.⁹⁸

The religious ideal that expected women to be so devoted to God as to be detached from their children was on display in this situation, nearly twelve hundred years after Paula and Jerome. Jane would have been familiar with Paula's experience and actions, including Paula's dry eyes as she sailed away from her children. Jane revealed that it was acceptable to be devoted to God *and* display emotional attachment to her children.

Over time and in cooperation with Francis, Jane established seventy religious communities and was responsible for overseeing them and keeping them connected.⁹⁹ Although this was not the original structure, eventually they were pressured by the bishop to become a "religious order observing enclosure and formal vows."¹⁰⁰ Despite those changes, Jane de

---

96. Wright, *Francis de Sales*, 59–60.

97. While we would rightly see this today as sexual abuse and Jane's daughter as a child bride, such cases are demonstrated throughout history. An "appropriate" age for marriage is a very recent concept. It should also be noted that arranged marriages have also been the historical norm.

98. Wright, *Francis de Sales*, 69–70.

99. Wright, "Salesian Spirituality."

100. Wright, *Francis de Sales*, 87.

Chantal not only found a way to live the life of a religious and of a mother, but she also paved the way for others to do the same.

On December 13, 1641, while suffering from an illness, "she asked the sisters to read to her Saint Jerome's account of the death of his spiritual friend Saint Paula, the record of Francis' own death . . . and Saint Augustine's relation of his mother's death. She passed away peacefully between six and seven in the evening that same day."[101] Her final requests to listen to both Saint Paula's and Saint Monica's accounts were fitting; as different as those two saints were in their mothering actions and religious life, Jane de Chantal managed to follow in both of their footsteps.

While Jane fulfilled the motherhood expectations of her time, even to the degree of caring for her father-in-law's other young children in addition to her own, she resisted remarriage as was expected of her. In addition, some of her mothering actions also would be unacceptable for today's mothering ideals. For example, sending a young son away to school was a common practice for the wealthy in Jane's day. However, even childcare utilized only while a mother works a day job is viewed with suspicion by today's motherhood standards. In addition, the idea of arranging a marriage for an eleven-year-old child bride is repugnant in today's American culture. However, it was an acceptable practice in Jane's time and culture. These exceptions aside, Jane did seek balance in her spiritual calling by creating a religious rule that allowed for family responsibilities. Her perspective understood the need for this allowance and inspired her to create this balance for others. We can also see her ministry in and among the convents she established as a form of mothering itself. This could be said of many of the mothers we have examined here. Jane de Chantal is another example of a mother in her specific circumstances making unique choices that resulted in unique mothering actions. For Jane de Chantal, as with the other women discussed above, there was not "one way" to mother.

SUSANNA WESLEY

Susanna Wesley was born in 1669 CE, to Samuel and Mary Annesley; Susanna was the daughter of a Puritan minister. Although there is no record of formal schooling for Susanna, it is apparent that she was educated during her early years. Although she would convert to the Church of England, "she drank deeply from the wells of English Puritanism and carried its

---

101. Wright, *Francis de Sales*, 115.

revolutionary spirit into her own home."[102] As a teenager, she met Samuel Wesley, and they married on November 11, 1688. He was twenty-six years old, and she was nineteen. Over time, Susanna would birth nineteen children; nine did not survive infancy. She was left with Samuel, Susanna, Emelia, Mary, Hetty, Anne, Martha, John, Charles, and Kezia. "Susanna turned her attention to the education of her children. . . . It was not at all customary to educate girls in that time, so it is remarkable that Susanna wanted not just her three sons, but all her children to be able to read, write, and reason well. . . . She also knew that above all she must teach her children to love God."[103] She established a consistent schooling schedule for her children, with three hours of study in the morning and another three in the afternoon every day but Sunday.[104]

An endearing practice of Susanna's demonstrates her commitment to the Christian discipline of prayer, paired with her busy mothering and homeschooling schedule: "Susanna would sometimes sit down and pull her apron over her head so that she could pray in peace. When she was thus accoutered, the children knew not to interrupt her."[105] Her spiritual practices eventually extended beyond her prayer time and spiritual leadership for her own family. While her rector husband was away, Susanna filled in, writing in a letter to him, "I cannot but look upon every soul you leave under my care as a talent committed to me under a trust by the great Lord of all the families."[106] She also began services in her own home on Sunday afternoons, initially for her children, reading sermons written by her husband or father. "Soon others began to ask if they could attend. Before long the house was crammed with scores of people wanting to hear Susanna read the sermons—more people than were attending church each week."[107] Eventually, complaints reached her out-of-town husband, stemming from the curate left in charge during Samuel's absence, who then wrote to his wife and requested she stop leading the Sunday afternoon services. Susanna disagreed with this request, as is evidenced in her reply: "If you do, after all, think fit to dissolve this assembly, do not tell me that you desire me to do it, for that will not satisfy my conscience: but send me your positive

---

102. Chilcote, *She Offered Them Christ*, 18.
103. Metaxas, *7 Women*, 37.
104. Metaxas, *7 Women*, 39.
105. Metaxas, *7 Women*, 41.
106. Chilcote, *She Offered Them Christ*, 19.
107. Metaxas, *7 Women*, 44.

command, in such full and express terms as may absolve me from all guilt and punishment for neglecting this opportunity of doing good when you and I shall appear before the great and awful tribunal of our Lord Jesus Christ."[108] As one author states, "Samuel wisely backed off,"[109] and Susanna continued her ministry.

Samuel and Susanna's children eventually lived a variety of different lives. All but Kezia married. A few had happy marriages, and several did not.[110] Most well-known of the children are John and Charles, who began the Methodist movement and became missionaries to America. Susanna is credited with influencing their education and spiritual formation, enabling them to become the leaders of this movement. It is possible that John's and Charles's history of encouraging women in leadership ministry positions within the Methodist movement may have been influenced by their mother's example. After she was widowed, Susanna lived with Emelia, then Samuel, then Martha and her husband, and eventually with John, where she stayed for the remainder of her life.[111]

Susanna has been held up as a positive example of a Christian mother, especially within the Wesleyan branches of church history. Like Dhuoda, Susanna prioritized Christian education for her children; she is an example of a woman who dedicated her life to her children and Christian ministry. Susanna technically followed her husband's leadership as complementarian theology stipulates, stating she would follow his wishes if he issued them as an absolute command. However, she is shown to push that boundary in her written reply asking for his clarification on her preaching.[112] Although John and Charles both were successful in Christian ministry, they and their siblings had their struggles. John is known to have had complicated romantic relationships, several sibling marriages were also difficult, and Hetty had

---

108. Chilcote, *She Offered Them Christ*, 20.

109. Chilcote, *She Offered Them Christ*, 20.

110. Metaxas, *7 Women*, 52–54.

111. Metaxas, *7 Women*, 55.

112. Although outside the scope of this book, female preachers were eventually "licensed" by John Wesley, and Wesleyan-Holiness denominations ordained women in the late 1800s, with Methodism following in the mid-twentieth century. Of course, preaching is also prohibited for women today in conservative/fundamentalist churches, which directly corresponds to a complementarian theology of marriage. Referencing 2 Tim 4:2, Piper and Grudem state, "The teaching prohibited to women here includes what we would call preaching . . . and the teaching of Bible and doctrine in the church, in colleges, and in seminaries." Piper and Grudem, *Recovering Biblical Manhood*, 181.

a child outside marriage, which was outside the accepted moral norms of the day. Susanna is credited with educating her children in general subjects such as reading and writing, and in the Christian faith. In many ways, she could be considered to have done everything "right" by today's motherhood standards. However, the fact that her children were not uniformly successful "model citizens" in their adult lives belies the contemporary ideal that assigns the psychological responsibility for children to their mother. The responsibility for unhappy relationships and an illegitimate child on the part of her adult children rests not on Susanna but on the actions of these adult children themselves. While Susanna evidenced strong Christian faith and ministry, as did Perpetua, Monica, Paula, Julian of Norwich, Dhuoda, and Jane de Chantal, she also forged her own mothering path, making choices in her specific circumstances that resulted in her own unique set of mothering actions. Susanna did not conform to established mothering expectations any more than these other maternal examples of Christian faith. As did the mothers before her, Susanna found her way to hear the word of God and do what it says.

SOJOURNER TRUTH

Sojourner Truth, whose given name was Isabella Baumfree, was born into slavery to James and Elizabeth Baumfree in Ulster County, New York, in 1797. She was sold several times, experiencing the hardship and cruel treatment of a child in slavery. "In those hours of her extremity, she did not forget the instructions of her mother, to go to God in all her trials, and every affliction; and she not only remembered, but obeyed: going to him, 'and telling him all—and asking Him if He thought it was right,' and begging him to protect and shield her from her persecutors."[113] Eventually, she was purchased by John Dumont.

"Around 1815, Truth fell in love with a slave named Robert from a neighboring farm. The two had a daughter, Diana."[114] She could not remain with Robert; instead, she was compelled by her owner "to marry an older slave named Thomas. The couple's marriage resulted in a son, Peter, and two daughters, Elizabeth and Sophia."[115] Motherhood for a woman in slavery came with challenges unheard of for mothers in any other position; she

---

113. Truth, *Narrative of Sojourner Truth*.
114. Truth, *Narrative of Sojourner Truth*.
115. Truth, *Narrative of Sojourner Truth*.

shared an example of this in her now-famous speech, "Ain't I a Woman," when she said, "I have borne thirteen children, and seen most all sold off to slavery, and when I cried out with my mother's grief, none but Jesus heard me!"[116] Another example of these challenges was demonstrated when her child and her mistress competed for her care; even when her child was crying, her mistress was cared for and her child was ignored, unless her master was bothered by the crying and intervened.[117]

"After John Dumont reneged on a promise to emancipate Truth in late 1826, she escaped to freedom with her infant daughter, Sophia. Her other daughter and son stayed behind."[118] She sought refuge with Isaac and Maria Van Wagener, who paid Dumont twenty dollars for the remaining year of her services, plus five dollars for the child.[119] Soon after, she discovered her five-year-old son Peter had been illegally sold to a slave owner in Alabama. With the help of the Van Wageners and the Quakers, Isabella took the illegal sale of Peter to court. She understood this was a risk and prayed "not only that her son might be returned, but that he should be delivered from bondage, and into her own hands, lest he should be punished out of mere spite to her."[120] There were several obstacles in this case, and when Peter was eventually returned to her, it was clear he had been severely abused in the intervening time. Her suit won out and the "case was one of the first in which a black woman successfully challenged a white man in a United States court."[121]

"On June 1, 1843, Isabella Baumfree changed her name to Sojourner Truth and devoted her life to Methodism and the abolition of slavery,"[122] alternately acting as a traveling preacher and supporting herself through domestic service. Sojourner is an example of a mother to whom today's motherhood standards do not apply. She was compelled to submit not to her husband but to whomever her owners were. She was compelled to marry a man of another's choosing and have children. However, she was

116. Sojourner Truth was not literate; written copies of her speeches are based on the memories of those who were in attendance when she spoke. This version of her famous "Ain't I a Woman?" speech was written twelve years after it was given. Truth only had five children, not thirteen. Truth, *Ain't I a Woman?*, 3.

117. Truth, *Narrative of Sojourner Truth*.
118. Truth, *Narrative of Sojourner Truth*.
119. Truth, *Narrative of Sojourner Truth*.
120. Truth, *Narrative of Sojourner Truth*.
121. Truth, *Narrative of Sojourner Truth*.
122. Truth, *Narrative of Sojourner Truth*.

not allowed to mother those children, forced to prioritize the care of her mistress. She shared, "I have had five children and never could take any one of them up and say 'my child' or 'my children,' unless it was when no one could see me."[123] Even the limited mothering she could provide ended abruptly as her children were sold away from her. This situation did not stop her fighting for them, as evidenced by her carrying her baby with her as she walked toward her freedom and when she sued for her son Peter. Sojourner's choices were greatly limited by her circumstances; she could not prioritize mothering over all else as today's motherhood ideology requires. As a Christian mother in a seemingly hopeless situation to which traditional motherhood could not adapt, Sojourner sought and recognized God's help in both mothering and Christian ministry. The accepted "one way" to mother did not extend to mothers in Sojourner's position. Nevertheless, Sojourner faithfully listened to and followed God's word. Of course, she is most known today for her radical speeches and activism for the causes of abolitionism and women's rights as first-wave feminism came on the scene. Certainly her misfortune and that of her children fueled the fire within her for both causes.

PHOEBE PALMER

A younger contemporary of Sojourner Truth, Phoebe Worrall was born to Methodist parents in New York City in 1807. In 1827 she married Walter Palmer, also a Methodist, and they attended Allen Street Methodist Church.[124] As was described in chapter 1, "It could be argued that almost any woman born in 1807 and living in upper-middle-class Victorian America would be shaped by the ideals set forth in the cult of domesticity, by the belief that the home was a most sacred space and utterly dependent on womanly virtues for its spiritual sustenance. Phoebe Palmer's rhetoric often supports this ideal of women's sphere."[125] This cultural assigning of spiritual virtue to women "led ultimately . . . to a conceptual enlargement of woman's sphere to include the church and society,"[126] certainly in Palmer's developing thought.

---

123. Truth, *Ain't I a Woman?*, 13.
124. Ingersol et al., *Our Watchword and Song*, 41–42.
125. Leclerc, *Singleness of Heart*, 107.
126. Leclerc, *Singleness of Heart*, 107.

Palmer's sphere grew beyond the home as she became a leader in the American Holiness Movement. Her experience as a mother informed her theology, sometimes in heartbreaking ways. She sadly experienced the deaths of three of her children in their infancy. She wrote, "After my loved ones were snatched away, I saw that I had concentrated my time and attention far too exclusively. . . . From henceforth, Jesus must and shall have the uppermost seat in my heart."[127] Although she did go on to have three other children, she never lost this perspective, considering anyone who may be prioritized in her heart or life over Christ to be idols. Palmer understood, as undoubtably many today and throughout history have understood, how easy it is for mothers to allow the great love for their children and family to take priority over all else. This allowance can include prioritizing children over their identities and their Christian faith. "For Phoebe Palmer . . . her 'own life' (her own ego, self-love, or pride) could have been more easily surrendered than her inordinate love for others, or relational idolatry."[128] In this understanding, "no longer is the home the means of personal piety; it has now become a potential spiritual hindrance."[129] Today's idealized standards and Christian complementarianism would seem to push "relational idolatry" as somehow holy, implying that God created gender hierarchy. Leclerc, interpreting Palmer, calls this sin.[130]

In seeking to overcome the relational idolatry of her children, "Abraham is often used as a model of faith in her letters and diaries, [Palmer] represents him as believing 'the promise' of God, but also as representing a deep trust in the person of God. This type of trust enabled Abraham to place Isaac 'on the altar,'"[131] signifying Abraham's sacrifice of his child to God as well as his trust in God. Palmer symbolically placed her children "on the altar" as well, signifying the same sacrifice and trust. "Consecration of other potential rivals for God's proper place in one's heart opens a person to the potential of holding a faith that expresses itself as entire devotion."[132] For Palmer, this consecration expressed itself not only in public ministry but

---

127. Wheatley, *Life and Letters*, ch. 1.
128. Leclerc, *Singleness of Heart*, 113.
129. Leclerc, *Singleness of Heart*, 122.
130. "Palmer's doctrine of original sin was not based on idolatry of self, but rather on relational idolatry. . . . This conceptional framing of *sin* allowed her to shift her perception of domestic responsibilities." Leclerc, *Singleness of Heart*, 121 (emphasis in original).
131. Leclerc, *Singleness of Heart*, 118.
132. Leclerc, *Singleness of Heart*, 118.

also in the domestic sphere. "Phoebe Palmer's view of original sin allowed her to spiritually detach herself from relational idols without dissolving the relationships themselves."[133]

Unlike other Christian mothers in history, Palmer did not need to physically leave her children behind, whether in martyrdom, pilgrimage, walking to freedom, or other circumstances. This entire devotion to God was a transformation of her heart that worked itself out in the context she already inhabited. Palmer confirmed that "'at this interesting point in her experience' she did not intend to 'neglect' the members of her family, but had only 'resolved that they should cease to be absorbing'—a disclaimer that reflected how aware she was of the domestic implications of her religious actions."[134]

At the same time, "if a woman professed entire devotion to God and counted herself free from idols and an absorption in domestic cares, she must be willing to do what God next asked of her, even if it went against social norms or protocol."[135] In the "cult of domesticity" era Palmer lived in, this did lead to countercultural actions on her part as well as that of other women. These actions and attitudes, which resulted from seeking God, from "hearing the word of God" and doing it, could also be considered countercultural in today's intensive mothering, complementarian context.

> It is crucial to see that for Palmer "self-sacrifice" did not mean playing the typical, martyr-like role of the subservient wife and mother.... It was a personal sacrifice for a woman to be considered "undignified" by society for overstepping her feminine boundaries. But such an undignified position, according to Palmer, was required by God. Rather than fulfilling their Christian responsibilities in the home alone, women were finding in Palmer's theology a religious imperative that necessitated a conceptual shift of women's calling and women's place.[136]

It is important to note that by inhabiting the roles of wife and mother while simultaneously proclaiming entire devotion to God, resulting in ministry outside the home that included preaching and extended travel, she validated, rather than dismissed, the importance of the domestic sphere. At the same time and with God's help, Palmer overcame the relational idolatry

---

133. Leclerc, *Singleness of Heart*, 122.
134. Hovet, "Palmer's 'Altar Phraseology,'" 272.
135. Leclerc, *Singleness of Heart*, 126.
136. Leclerc, *Singleness of Heart*, 126.

Mothering, God, and the Mothering God

that came naturally to her, that of placing her children first in her heart and life. She did this in a cultural context that encouraged this idolatry, holding it up as a sign of her true womanhood and her true calling as a Christian woman. Likewise, today's culture holds up the idolatry of intensive and complementarian mothering as signs of a good mother, affirming these ideals as a mother's true calling as a Christian. While Palmer recognized the value of mothering, she also recognized the greater importance of putting God first in her heart. Palmer placed her identity not in mothering but rather in Christ.

As stated above, today's intensive mothering would have contemporary mothers believe there is one way to mother and one way to mother as a Christian; anyone who falls outside of those norms is perceived to fail as a "good" mother. Each woman discussed in this chapter found a different balance as a Christian mother, each taking different mothering actions. Each woman prioritized Christian service and the responsibilities of caring for their children in ways fitting to their personality and situation. Although regarded by the Christian church as exemplary Christians, none fully fit within the bounds of patriarchal motherhood. Perpetua witnessed through martyrdom, Monica evangelized her son, Paula gave up her children for God, and Dhuoda educated and advised. Julian wrote of God's motherhood, Jane balanced motherhood of children with motherhood of a religious order, Susanna taught and preached, and Sojourner fought for freedom. Phoebe laid her children on the symbolic altar, began to preach, and birthed a movement that calls her its matriarch. Some mothered primarily within the patriarchal motherhood framework, some left this framework behind, and some did not ever fit within that framework. All followed God. Whether or not they may have measured up to today's motherhood standards as "good" mothers, they each are revealed as women who were exemplary Christians. While there is not "one way" to mother, each of these mothers found her way to hear the word of God and do what it says.

5

Relevant Ramifications for Today's Church

IMAGINE THE FOLLOWING SCENARIO in which a couple attends church for the first time in years. What is their motivation, how would their experience unfold, and what impressions would they carry with them afterward? The account below is fictional but based on real events observed in evangelical worship services in contemporary America.

Chloe was at her breaking point. Mostly, she was exhausted. Her full-time job kept her busy, but she had enjoyed being active for years. It wasn't until the birth of her first child four years ago that she began to feel overextended. Now, she had a full-time job, a four-year-old son, Cayden, and an eighteen-month-old daughter, Mia. Her husband Marc was sympathetic but slightly mystified by her situation. As an "involved father," he helped at home, sharing some of the housework and occasionally bedtime routines. Still, the responsibility to keep everything going, from childcare to scheduling to remembering to take out the garbage, fell on Chloe. There was always more to do, and although Marc found time to relax most evenings, Chloe couldn't seem to make this happen. She missed having downtime or any time at all for self-care. She was embarrassed to admit how long it had been since she had gone for a run, once a staple in her routine. She knew this was part of her inability to lose her baby weight and her continued "baby blues," over a year past the point she should be experiencing them, but she couldn't squeeze time for exercise into her schedule.

These issues were part of why she was motivated enough to convince her husband to try out church this past Sunday. Although they had both attended as children, Marc had phased out of attending church during his teenage years, and Chloe followed suit once she left home for college. By the time they met and married several years later, church had been a distant memory. However, Chloe recalled feeling close to God during some youth group meetings and remembered how encouraging those moments had been. When she realized she needed help, those memories prompted hope that a return to church might provide it. It had been close to a decade since she had been to a worship service and even longer for Marc. Chloe began to review their recent church experience as she drove to pick up their children after work.

As they pulled into the church parking lot, the name of the male pastor and the service times were listed on the digital reader board. The screen flashed to the next frame, which read, "He who is born of God will resemble his Father." Marc and Chloe had joked about how Chloe might begin to look like her dad, thankful that although she had a similar "tummy pooch," she hadn't started to grow facial hair. This conversation brought questions from Cayden, wondering if his sister Mia would also develop a beard, prompting a smothered giggle and a rushed explanation from Chloe. At first, Chloe thought their exchange might make a cute social media post but then changed her mind, thinking of the backlash she was sure to receive from her progressively-minded friends. This train of thought left her feeling unsure about the exclusive language used on the sign, but she shook it off, hopeful for a meaningful morning.

The greeters in the church lobby were friendly and helpful, showing them the way to the nursery and how to check in on the computerized system. Chloe was invited to a moms' group that meets on a weekday morning, which she won't be able to attend because of her job. She appreciated the warm invitation but wondered if it was assumed that all mothers stay home with their children. Marc noticed there were no other men in the nursery and felt out of place, commenting to Chloe that next time he would wait in the hall until she was done. This was not as unsettling as it might have been, Chloe reflected at the time, since she was usually the parent to handle childcare drop-offs and pick-ups during the week. However, Chloe decided to keep this thought to herself, having previously received

Relevant Ramifications for Today's Church

the "I-don't-want-someone-else-to-raise-my-children" mentality toward childcare. She suspected the friendly nursery volunteers might have that same mentality as if, by utilizing their carefully chosen learning center, Chloe and Marc weren't the ones raising their children. Paid childcare was part of their family's "village" but not everyone understood that. With that potentially awkward social situation skirted, and feeling confident in the level of care Cayden and Mia would receive, Chloe and Marc found their way to the sanctuary.

As the musical intro played, Chloe and Marc used the QR code from the screen up front to pull up the church's website. The website was contemporary, in contrast to the archaic language of the verse from John 3:3 written across the top of the home page, which read, "Except a man be born again, he cannot see the Kingdom of God" (KJV). Chloe knew the New Testament enough to understand this includes her, but she had to consciously include herself because the language did not.

The morning's worship songs included hymns familiar to both Chloe and Marc, and contemporary choruses new to them. However, since Chloe had noticed the male-dominant language used on both the outside reader board and the church website, she couldn't help seeing the proliferation of male-dominated language in the song selection. She wasn't surprised at this language in the hymns, although she considered such language dated, as she remembered some of the hymns from childhood. However, she was caught off guard by the supposedly "contemporary" choruses and their over-use of male terms such as "he," "his," "Father," "King," or "Sons of God," alongside the absence of equivalent female-oriented or gender-neutral terms. Even Marc had sarcastically joked about "coming to the right place" when he noticed that the church staff and all the ushers were male.

Chloe had reflected at the time that her job in communications had made her more aware of the impact of words and presentation and decided to dismiss her unease, at least for the time, in the hopes of an uplifting sermon. However, she realized she would have to hold out a little longer when the scripture passage and the pastoral prayer were again filled with male-dominated language. She noticed that Marc was also becoming uncomfortable when he made another joke, this time about the phrase "Father we just" used repeatedly in the prayer. He asked Chloe if she had ever encountered the new term "fatherwejus" as she edited online content at work. While Chloe had snorted at his whispered humor, she wondered where either of them would be without their mothers as well as their fathers, questioning why mothers were not also deemed an appropriate metaphor for God.

Although Chloe had been hoping for encouragement through the sermon, she did not receive it. If anything, she reflected as she drove; the sermon had been a source of *dis*couragement instead. The text had been from Matt 14, in which five thousand men were mentioned, but the "women and children" had been tossed in with a "besides"; the pastor had not done anything to help make these invisible persons seen. The pastor continued the male-dominated language of the first half of the service, and Chloe felt progressively more invisible and dismissed. "Laymen," "forefathers," and "the inner man" were each referenced, along with the continued male language used of God. There were quotes from male theologians and references to football, auto repairs, and hunting, which, although they technically could be female-oriented activities, added to Chloe's feelings of invisibility; she began to feel in earnest that she did not belong. She wondered what happened to the illustrations used by Jesus, such as cleaning the house, mending clothes, or caring for children. The only comments that came close were regarding the pastor's wife, whose life purpose was presented as supporting the pastor.

Between the nursery check-in, the messaging in the service, and the pastor's comments, Chloe began feeling the additional burden of supporting her children and husband, thinking she needed to spend more time becoming a better wife and mother. This brought her up short, however, as she couldn't imagine how she would manage more time to devote to them when she already lacked the time for a full night's sleep. The thought of less sleep than she was currently getting was the reality check she needed; Chloe supported her family and had come to church that morning hoping for some support for herself. Marc also seemed to be reaching the end of his patience with the service. Now past the joking phase, he reminded her that a pope had once said, "Only men may truly represent Christ here on earth," and asked Chloe if that is what this church believed too. Not long after that, they slipped out of the back of the sanctuary, and Chloe went to pick up their children, with Marc waiting in the hall as promised.

As Chloe neared the end of their drive home, she reflected on how easy it was to get pulled into guilt-induced expectations. Although she couldn't name it, Chloe had begun to reawaken to faith and had been hopeful for a renewed relationship with God through church involvement. After her recent experience, however, she reflected that although she was still exhausted and overwhelmed, the church would likely not be the encouragement she had hoped for. Instead, she had felt alienated and burdened with guilt, and she concluded that she must have imagined the spiritual experiences she remembered from her teenage years. Chloe took a deep breath and mentally prepared to pick up her high-energy children and the start of her "second shift."[1]

Mothers today have been sold a false narrative, as have their families and the American culture. This narrative convincingly implies that a mother's primary purpose is to fulfill the impossible cultural ideals of intensive motherhood. This narrative reinforces the idea that women who are mothers will live happy and fulfilled lives only if they live up to these motherhood standards. This narrative also implies that the same is true of their children: children will only live happy and fulfilled lives if their mothers live up to these standards. This adds to the motherhood burden. Although complementarian expectations oppose biblical and historical examples, complementarian ideals are often layered in with these motherhood standards; this remains especially true within the church. These unrealistic cultural expectations are not solely a patriarchal construct; mothers often reinforce and build on this ideal. Read any current book, article, blog, or tweet authored by a mother on mothering and the message is surprisingly consistent: yes, mothering is exceedingly difficult, but it is "worth it." It is hard, but there is meaning and joy in mothering. Popular media powerfully heightens and reinforces this message.

MOTHERING TODAY

The element that makes this line of thought almost impossible to refute is that, overall, it is true; mothering is "worth it." There is often joy and meaning in the mothering experience. Mothering is essential and should not be dismissed. From a theological perspective, although God did not create women solely to be mothers to the exclusion of everything else, and God did not create women to be subservient mothers, God did create women capable of becoming mothers. While this capability is not the whole, it is part of women being equally created in the image of God. God as Mother sets this example in God's life-giving acts of creation and mothering. Like

1. Several points in this story are updated and adapted from another account of a first-time church visit found in Smith, *Is It Okay*, 14–18.

Eve, mothers co-create with God. The intense love mothers have for their children, a love that reflects God's love, has been inappropriately paired with today's mothering ideals. This has secured intensive mothering a place in today's society.

Intensive mothering is often paired with complementarian mothering within the evangelical church. Intensive mothering is also paired with unequal parenting standards for mothers and fathers, inside and outside the church. This pairing often results in mothers committing to living up to these unrealistic motherhood standards, often at the expense of their own careers, health, relationships, personal identities, and even their own spiritual formation. Inside and outside the Christian church,

> both intensive mothering and the idea of motherhood as a difficult choice have deeply shaped the way women talk about their experiences. Mothers continue to tell researchers that their children and their choices as mothers anchor their identities. This is generally true across lines of class and race and mothers' employment status. . . . Women who see themselves as good mothers say they are intensely involved with their children, available to them, and self-sacrificing. It is clear that they invest themselves deeply in maternal identities.[2]

Some women identify as mothers to such a degree that there is neither time nor room in their lives to form any other identity; this includes identity in Christ. This primary identification as mothers is the case despite examples to the contrary set by women in the Bible and throughout history. Many of these biblical and historical examples of positive mothering have been misrepresented or forgotten by the church, often including those discussed in this book, exacerbating this problem. The result is congregations unaware of these powerful mothering examples. Mothers cannot follow examples of which they are unaware. Women with children form primary identities as mothers, unaware of any other option as Christian mothers.

Not only have women been conditioned by society to form their identities as mothers to the exclusion of all else, but they have also been discipled by the church to mother in this way. Mothers have been discipled to shape their lives in this way. This form of maternal discipleship even occurs within churches that do not officially subscribe to complementarian theology, (such as the Church of the Nazarene and other Holiness groups). This form of relational idolatry is a blind spot in today's evangelical Christian

---

2. Vandenberg-Daves, *Modern Motherhood*, 267.

faith because Christians have been taught that this type of mothering is a good and honorable goal for Christian mothers. They have been taught that for Christian mothers, this is what matters most. They have further been taught that what matters most for Christian mothers is *how* they mother and that this is the "one way" to mother. As a result, the conservative church has often produced disciples of intensive, complementarian motherhood rather than disciples of Christ. The church has discipled mothers, fathers, families, and everyone else in this ideology; the church has accepted this false narrative and worked to reinforce it. Entire families believe that for mothers to be "good Christians," they must be "good mothers" according to today's motherhood standards. However, it would be inaccurate to say that there is no overlap and that women and families who strive to adhere to these ideologies are not Christians. It also does not mean that women who reach for intensive mothering standards are not simultaneously sincerely seeking Christ or that God cannot be found within intensive motherhood. However, it does highlight the issue that often Christian American families mirror American society's intensive motherhood standards, not despite the church's teachings but instead, because they have incorrectly been discipled by the church to do so.

The issue of intensive, complementarian mothering is more than a "mother's issue." It is also more than a family issue or a women's issue; it is a discipleship issue. Until intensive, complementarian motherhood is addressed and resolved, women will continue to be viewed and treated as less-than-equal, including women who are pastors and leaders within the church. Unrealistic motherhood standards apply to female pastors and church leaders just as they apply to women in any other life situation. These expectations also have the potential to prevent women from acquiring the expertise to become pastors and leaders within the church in the first place. The impact of motherhood expectations on church leaders and members affects the church as a whole and, by extension, society as a whole. In addition, these expectations, and the resulting treatment of mothers, deprive all people, female and male alike, of a fuller understanding of God. If a true mother can only be an intensive, complementarian mother, the world is robbed of understanding God as Mother, as the two viewpoints are incompatible. The world is also robbed of understanding women as entirely created in God's image. This less-than-equal viewpoint further deprives churches of an egalitarian Christian community in which all persons contribute with God-given giftings, free from the restraints of patriarchal society.[3]

Where does the evangelical church go from here? Nothing less than a full-scale culture change within the church can alter these perceptions. Further, this cultural change within the church will necessarily be countercultural to today's secular society rather than mirroring it as it does now. Addressing every detail of this sort of large-scale change within the Christian church is beyond the scope of this book. Instead, this project is intended as a conversation starter, with the hope that others will add ideas, insights, and ultimately, solutions to the issues raised here. To further this conversation, some questions churches can ask themselves regarding this topic are discussed below. These questions cover a lot of "little" things and a few "big" things, which combined have the potential to contribute to a shift in perceptions of mothering within church culture. These questions are not exhaustive; more will be needed to shift these deeply ingrained beliefs. However, they hopefully offer a viable starting point.

BIBLICAL TEACHING

Church leadership can begin by examining what the local church is overtly teaching. For example, what topics do sermons cover, which biblical characters, situations, and metaphors are presented, and how are they presented? Representation of women and mothers matter, both within and outside the church context. Next, preach and teach on the principles discussed in this book. Address the passages used to press women into the complementarian mold of submissive wives and mothers, using accurate exegesis to refute complementarian claims. Next, clarify what these passages mean for mothers, families, relationships, and how all the above interact with each other and God. Finally, use sermons, small groups, Bible studies, classes, printed and electronic publications, and online forums such as live streams, blogs, and social media to teach the mothers and mothering metaphors examined here, including God as Mother.

Churches can consider whether women, including mothers, are presented as entirely created in the image of God. When mothers and women are addressed in biblical teaching, are they presented accurately? Is Eve

---

3. It is important to note that while it is true this issue extends beyond those who are mothers, were it an issue that affected only mothers, it would still be an issue imperative to address.

represented as the archetype of the first sinful temptress, or is she understood in all her adult complexity, both unwise yet growing, co-creating with God? Do Sarah and Hagar demonstrate unrealistic matriarchal ideals, or do they demonstrate God's working in complicated, messy lives, lives involving incest, trafficking, abuse, abandonment, fierce mothering, and theophany? Is Rebekah understood as an interfering, manipulative mother or as the faith leader she was, acting outside of male headship to work out God's plan? Are Leah, Rachel, Bilhah, and Zilpah allowed to share their complicated, true-to-modern-life stories of longing, rejection, abuse, oppression, rivalry, and blended family complications, or are they instead forced into a happier but unrealistic mold reflecting white-washed versions of motherhood? Is Hannah allowed to sing for justice as Mary did while simultaneously longing for and giving up her child? Or is she instead pressed into a motherhood ideal in which she does not fit? Is Mary portrayed as the slightly confused, sentimentalized, virgin mother, restricted to Christmas and Easter, or is she allowed to emerge through the biblical text as the full-of-grace theologian, prophet, and disciple she was? What of other biblical mothers not mentioned in this book, such as Moses's mothers, Tamar, Ruth, Bathsheba, Rizpah, Samson's mother, the Canaanite woman, Zebedee's wife, and more? What of metaphorical mothers such as Deborah, Rachel as she weeps for her children, Zion, or the apostle Paul?

While representation is important, it is essential that such representation accurately represents what the Bible contains. When passages on mothers and mothering are misrepresented, they harm the church body, as complementarian teaching on such passages has done. However, when presented correctly, these passages have the power of Scripture to teach, reprove, correct, and train in righteousness.[4] The church body needs this kind of biblically accurate representation and loses out on the fullness of Scripture when it is absent.

When the stories of biblical mothers are taught to church congregations, are they represented as examples for the entire congregation or just for a segment of the congregation? For example, in chapter 4, Phoebe Palmer referenced Abraham as an example for herself as a mother. If Phoebe as a woman could look to a biblical man as an example for her life, could biblical women be used as examples for men's lives as well as for women's? In addition to Abraham, could Sarah similarly be referenced as an example for the entire congregation, both mothers and fathers, women and men?

---

4. See 2 Tim 3:16.

Could other biblical women be referenced in this same way? Are biblical examples used to speak honestly about God's work in the world and the lives of people today, freeing mothers, and by extension, fathers and others, to live as God has created and called them? Or are these examples instead inappropriately used to reinforce intensive mothering and complementarian ideals? Biblical characters and metaphors, the way they are represented by the church, and who they are represented to and for, can set the tone for equal, appropriate gender roles and expectations in the larger church culture and beyond. The evangelical church can benefit from setting this tone through presenting biblical mothers and mothering metaphors to and for all persons rather than restricting this teaching to women or mothers.

LANGUAGE, SYMBOLS, AND SONG

What language is used of God? Is God referred to only in male terms such as "Father" and with only male pronouns? In addition to using these male metaphors, could female metaphors such as "Mother" and female pronouns of God also make an appearance from the pulpit? "There is widespread agreement among Christian theologians that God transcends gender, but our pronouns speak louder than our theology and our qualifications. How will anyone believe us when we say that God both encompasses and transcends male and female if we talk as if God is only male?"[5] What biblical pictures of God are presented in sermons and Bible studies? Are passages that portray God as Mother allowed to speak accurately, or are they glossed over, sentimentalized, or avoided altogether? God as a nursing mother in place of Moses, God as Warrior and Woman-in-Labor, God as Artisan and Laboring Woman, God as more loving than a nursing mother, and Jesus as Mother are all powerful images essential to a complete understanding of God. Are the maternal aspects in metaphors that reference God's work, such as labor, breastfeeding (milk), new life, new birth, and being born again, recognized as maternal? Beyond the examples explored in this book, are the many references to God's feeding and provision or maternal love throughout the Bible recognized as the motherly references that they are? While this usage extends beyond the "mother" metaphor, it speaks to women, and therefore mothers, being fully and equally created in the image of God. It also speaks to all of God's children, female and male, with the understanding that this female image is also a reflection of God. As

---

5. Smith, *Is It Okay*, 39.

previously noted, the maternal understanding of God reveals intensive and complementarian motherhood as the limiting, unbiblical understanding of mothering that it is. Rightly understanding the maternal and paternal anthropomorphisms of God has great theological import extending beyond human reflections of God. Bulkeley reminds us,

> The creator of the universe is neither a father nor a mother. God neither fathered the world by impregnating someone or something, nor gave birth to the world. God created it from nothing. This is why the image of God is not in either man or woman alone, but male and female together (Genesis 1:27). If this is true, then to worship God as a father alone is to worship something that is less than the creator of all. The god that we would be worshiping in that case is a god that we have created for ourselves, not the biblical God. This is idolatry.[6]

Is the church mindful of avoiding this form of idolatry, or is it promoting idolatry through its language of God? Consider how this language affects our worship of God and understanding of each other. How does our language of God build or reinforce our understanding and expectation of others, created in God's image, including mothers? The church can be intentional to avoid this form of idolatry and tap into the abundance of rich language found in biblical, female, and maternal metaphors of God. These steps have the potential to help worshipers in their understanding of God, each other, and community, and deepen worship of God.

What language is used of the congregation and community? Is it assumed that women are included in male pronouns, or are women intentionally included in the language utilized? Simple examples of this language could include using the term *humankind* rather than *mankind*, *person* rather than *man*, or *parent* rather than *mother* or *father*. "It is estimated that the average person comes into contact with the generic 'he' more than 10 million times during the course of a lifetime. And each time, men are subtly reminded that women don't count, and women are told to find their identity in men."[7] Smith shares that many Christians "have yet to take the first step toward relating to women as equals with men, and changing their language about persons accordingly."[8] A part of teaching that all persons are created in the image of God includes the language used of all people. Is the

---

6. Bulkeley, *Not Only a Father*, 96.
7. Ng, "Androcentric Coding," 455; Smith, *Is It Okay*, 32.
8. Smith, *Is It Okay*, 261.

church affirming the truth that all people are created equally in the image of God through its language, or is church language rendering part of the congregation invisible? Is the church teaching equality through language, or instead, is it teaching unrecognized but systemic oppression? Specific to this book, does church language validate women who are mothers, or does it instead reinforce inappropriate stereotypes of the silent, submissive wife and mother of complementarian legend? The church, including the conservative evangelical church, has a responsibility to represent scripture accurately, not only in what it teaches but also in the language it uses.

What Bible translations are used for teaching and preaching? What translations are recommended to church congregants? The language of the Bible itself matters when it comes to the correct portrayal of biblical mothers. Biblical language in the translations utilized by churches communicates how women and mothers are viewed. "The context in which all the early modern English Bibles arose championed a language that excluded women. The emphasis on masculine language continued throughout English Bibles. . . . From this perspective, gender-inclusive language isn't distorting Scripture. Gender-inclusive language is restoring Scripture from the influence of certain English Bible translations."[9] This is important, as "the English Bible translated more than Hebrew text; it also translated early modern English ideas about marriage into biblical text, as well as a 'falsely universal language' that excluded women. . . . Because women were written out of the early English Bible, modern evangelicals have more easily written women out of church leadership."[10] Modern evangelicals have also more easily written women exclusively into complementarian wife and mother roles. Again, the church has a responsibility to represent scripture accurately; this accurate representation includes not just teaching on the ideas put forth in scripture but also in the language of that scripture and the meaning behind the language.

Note whether the intentionally egalitarian language in the church extends beyond words spoken by the main speaker or preacher to include written language and language used in song. Smith recommends, "Ask your church worship leaders to stop singing songs that use gender-exclusive language for persons. Or to not sing those verses which contain such language.

---

9. Barr, *Making of Biblical Womanhood*, 148.

10. Barr, *Making of Biblical Womanhood*, 150. For a full discussion on how English Bible translations were created and their effect on women, see Barr's chapter on the topic, "Writing Women Out of the English Bible," in Barr, *Making of Biblical Womanhood*, 129–50.

Or re-write any phrases or lines in hymns that use gender exclusive language. . . . This says we are willing to take a public stand against sexist language."[11] In a further bid against sexist language, is this language recognized and called out when it appears in church and society, whether sung, written, or spoken? "It's one thing to say that all people are of equal value. It's another to talk about sexism and call it sin."[12] In the same vein, it is one thing to talk about putting God first in our lives and identities. It's another to talk about relational idolatry as it manifests in intensive mothering and complementarianism and call it sin. These steps contribute to the overall culture of the church and set expectations for church members.

Beyond language, what symbols are a part of worship? William Willimon explains,

> Social change is primarily symbolic change. In order for us to change, our symbols must change. Our symbols must change because they determine our horizons, our limits, our viewpoints and visions. . . . Symbolic change needed to be made in order to adjust the metaphors and symbols to the church's clear vision of the role of women in the church. We realize how limited many of our old, male-dominated, hierarchical images were—God the Father; the Heavenly King; Lord over All; Rise Up, O Men of God. There could be no basic change without change in the symbols and metaphors through which we attempt to grasp reality and reality grasps us.
>
> The liturgy reminds us that we are more image-making and image-using creatures than we think. We apprehend reality only through symbols, sacraments, gestures, and metaphor.[13]

What symbols and language, whether spoken, written, or sung, form worship and culture within the church? How do these symbols and language affect attitudes within the church, and how do they affect mothers and other persons within the church? It is important for the church to be aware of the impactful role symbols and language have in setting its culture. It is also important for the church to be intentional in its use of both symbols and language to create a culture that speaks to the fullness of God, rather than limiting symbols to represent a masculine God and male congregants. It is further important for the church to create a culture that affirms all persons,

---

11. Smith, *Is It Okay*, 263–64. For examples of re-written language, such as using *church* or *saints* in place of *men*, see Smith, *Is It Okay*, 264.

12. Smith, *Is It Okay*, 259.

13. Willimon, *Service of God*, 57.

female and male, as equally created in the image of God. Although this is a larger issue, for the purpose of this book, this overall culture is important in the expectations it sets in the hearts and minds of all church attenders toward the role of women and mothers in church and society.

CHURCH LEADERSHIP, WOMEN'S MINISTRIES, AND WOMEN MINISTERS

In addition to symbols, language, and song, who is standing in the pulpit or at the head of the Bible class? When only men are authorized to preach or are the only persons authorized to teach and lead other men, as is the case with complementarian theology, "the unspoken message is that while women benefit from learning from both sexes, men cannot be taught or enriched by women. . . . Why is that? In Scripture itself, we see men learning plenty from women."[14] What messages are communicated about the role of women and mothers in the church and society by the simple act of who is authorized to share the Word publicly? Further, are examples of biblical mothers and mothering metaphors, when utilized, limited to a female guest speaker, sermons on Mother's Day, or teachings about Mary during Advent? Do they instead extend into the regular rotation of preaching, presented not as a "special event" or "token sermon about women" but instead as part of the more extensive dialogue involved in "hearing the Word," presented for everyone as part of daily Christian life? If these examples are shared from the pulpit, do they extend beyond that? Are Bible study leaders and Sunday school teachers educated and comfortable facilitating and teaching on these topics, using appropriate language and accurate portrayals of biblical passages? If they are not, is training available to educate and encourage leaders in this direction? Those setting church practice can take intentional steps to normalize women in leadership, teaching, and preaching roles and the use of biblical examples of women and mothers in its theological education. Again, although this kind of normalization is a move in the right direction on the larger issue of equality in the church; it is also an essential piece of the puzzle in addressing the problems of intensive mothering and complementarian theology.

Determine what classes and programs are offered by the local church, for whom, and what topics are covered. Are women included in meaningful ministries, or are they relegated to "specialty" programs centering around

14. Byrd, *Recovering from Biblical Manhood*, ch. 1.

topics that do not require the "leadership" of men? For example, the strong history of women leading missions societies in many church denominations was intentionally transitioned away from missions and into women's ministries in recent decades. "By the 1970s and 1980s . . . female missionary societies—for so long the domain of independent and, often husbandless, women—had been gutted as an ecclesiastical force."[15]

> As historian Elizabeth Flowers has chronicled, the energy once invested in their missionary enterprise was later channeled into the new anti-feminist cause as "women's ministry." In 1980, Joyce Rogers hosted four thousand women . . . [to] "encourage women in fulfilling their traditional roles as wives and mothers as well as challenge women to become involved in promoting moral virtue and traditional family values in our society."[16]

Rather than pursuing missionary endeavors, topics at women's ministry events such as this included "color coordination," "makeup," "nutrition," "gracious hostess and etiquette," "praise in the dance," and "on being a pastor's wife."[17] Susie Hawkins, former pastor's wife at megachurch First Baptist in Dallas, shared, "It was a lot more fun than talking about missions, that's for sure. Those poor missionary societies. They never stood a chance."[18]

While Holiness denominations and others did not dissolve women's involvement in their missionary endeavors, it was nonetheless affected by this shift in church culture.[19] The Nazarene denomination, for example,

15. Bowler, *Preacher's Wife*, ch. 2.

16. Bowler, *Preacher's Wife*, ch. 2.

17. These were the women's seminar choices for the 1985 National Leadership Conference. See Bowler, *Preacher's Wife*, ch. 2.

18. Bowler, *Preacher's Wife*, ch. 2.

19. The Woman's Missionary Society (WMS) was founded in April 1899, and recognized as an auxiliary organization of the Church of the Nazarene in 1915. In 1952, the WMS changed its name to the Nazarene Foreign Missionary Society, "reflecting the introduction of men, youth, and children into the organization." See Church of the Nazarene, "Nazarene Missions." Although "women always had ministered as ordained elders in the Church of the Nazarene," "controlled the missionary society," "served with particular freedom on mission fields," "made up twelve percent of Nazarene pastors in 1925," and often pastored and taught alongside their pastor-husbands, "Nazarenes increasingly emphasized a domestic and less public role for women. To an extent, this was a reaction to the feminist movement sweeping in the United States. In 1975 there were only eighty-two women pastors (2 percent of the total number of pastors) and forty-five women serving as evangelists in North America. Women had made up 43 percent of the denomination's evangelists in 1908 and 23 percent in 1945 but only 9 percent in 1975." Ingersol et al., *Our Watchword and Song*, 429, 432.

embraced women's ministries in addition to missions and channeled significant energy in that direction; the remains of these women's ministries are still active today. Are they effective? Are they providing women with a meaningful place to connect, serve, and lead? While these changes did not target women who were mothers to the exclusion of other women, mothers were included in this "women's ministry" change. What are women's ministries across churches and denominations teaching, both through implicit and explicit means, about the role of women and mothers in church and society? Are they empowering women to hear the word of God and do it fully, or are they encouraging women to conform to the "one way" of intensive and complementarian motherhood standards instead? Women's ministries groups and their teaching within churches are set up as the authority on how women are to live out their lives as Christians; these are the Christian women held up as examples for other women within the church. Because they have such strong influence, it is important for women's groups within churches to examine their messaging carefully. Do they recognize the difference between complementarianism and equality within marriage? This messaging appears both through stated goals and explicit communications, and through the messages that activities, programming, teaching, and group culture communicates. The messaging of women's ministries is a powerful tool within churches to disciple women and mothers toward Christ rather than in intensive mothering or complementarian ideologies.

Some of today's remaining women's ministry programs include moms' groups, women's Bible studies, and even study Bibles specifically marketed to women and mothers. These can be valuable ministries if led appropriately. However, in addressing separate Bibles marketed to women, mothers, and men, author Aimee Byrd comments, "The specific articles targeted to the women's Bible predominantly address weakness and victimhood while the men's are about leadership and agency. The ones that do address a man's weakness are focused on how they victimize women."[20] She further questions, "Do women have nothing to learn about leadership, self-control, calling, and life in the local church? Do men not need to learn about forgiveness, emotional health, and missional living?"[21] She concludes, "The underlying message is that there is a men's version and a woman's version to read. There is a male and a female way to meditate on the Bible's teaching.

---

20. Byrd, *Recovering from Biblical Manhood*, ch. 1.
21. Byrd, *Recovering from Biblical Manhood*, ch. 1.

And this separates the sexes by our cultural gender paradigms."[22] This author suspects many of the same comments could be made about the topics addressed in separate women's and men's Bible studies, women's and men's church activities, and specialty moms' groups within churches. The apparent conclusion contradicting this line of thought is that there is one Holy Bible for all members of the church community, the entire contents intended for every believer. Specific Scriptures are not intended for one group of people and not another.[23]

The way church congregations view mothers is strongly intertwined with the way church congregations view women in ministry leadership, including female teachers and pastors. As long as mothers are burdened with the unrealistic expectations of intensive mothering and complementarianism, women in church leadership will be burdened with the same. Further, the same complementarian concepts that confine women to the roles of submissive wife and mother also prohibit women from leadership positions in the church. Likewise, the banning of women from ministry leadership positions in the church reinforces the complementarian agenda that restricts women to the roles of submissive wife and mother. Therefore, it is worth a brief look at the biblical basis for women in ministry leadership.

The primary argument for women in ministry leadership within the Christian church today is the occurrence of women in ministry leadership in the Christian church in the Bible. One example is in Rom 16:1–15, where the apostle Paul shares a commendation and greetings to a list of Christian believers. Beth Allison Barr clarifies the women in this list:

> Phoebe, the deacon who carried the letter from Paul and read it aloud to her house church.
>
> Prisca (Priscilla), whose name is mentioned before her husband's name (something rather notable in the Roman world) as a co-worker with Paul.
>
> Mary, a hard worker for the gospel in Asia.
>
> Junia, prominent among the apostles.
>
> Tryphaena and Tryphosa, Paul's fellow workers in the Lord.
>
> The beloved Persis, who also worked hard for the Lord.

22. Byrd, *Recovering from Biblical Manhood*, ch. 1.

23. An exception may be children who are too young for some biblical topics; even then, age-appropriate teachings can be found or created.

Mothering, God, and the Mothering God

Rufus's mother, Julia, and Nereus's sister.

Ten women recognized by Paul.

Seven women are recognized by their ministry: Phoebe, Priscilla, Mary, Junia, Tryphaena, Tryphosa, and Persis. One woman, Phoebe, is identified as a deacon. . . . Another woman, Junia, is identified not simply as an apostle but as one who was prominent among the apostles.[24]

These women, commended and greeted by Paul, not only represent biblical women in ministry leadership, they also help clarify 1 Cor 14:34–35 and 1 Tim 2:11–12. These two passages, written by Paul, have been misinterpreted to portray the apostle as prohibiting all women from ministry leadership in all situations. Although this seems to be in contrast to his biblical list of women in ministry, it is important to recognize that "Paul isn't inconsistent in his approach to women; we have made him inconsistent through how we have interpreted him. As Romans 16 makes clear, the reality is that biblical women contradict modern ideas of [complementarianism.]"[25] In fact, "Paul is not limiting women's leadership; he tells us with his own hand that women lead in the early church and that he supports their ministries."[26] It is not the Bible that is incorrect; it is the interpretations that claim certain passages prohibit women from ministry leadership that are incorrect. A closer examination of these passages is warranted.

First Corinthians 14:34–35 reads, "Women should be silent in the churches. For they are not permitted to speak, but should be subordinate, as the law also says. If there is anything they desire to know, let them ask their husbands at home. For it is shameful for a woman to speak in church." Again, it is clear from Paul's writings that these verses were not intended to be universally applied. C. Jeanne Orjala Serrão underscores this point by writing, "Context is very important to even begin to understand this passage because, first of all, just three chapters earlier in 1 Corinthians 11, Paul tells us that men and women are praying and prophesying (preaching) in the church! So which is it? Women praying and prophesying, or women being silent? It cannot be both!"[27]

---

24. Barr, *Making of Biblical Womanhood*, 64–65. Most, if not all, of the mothers discussed in chapter 4 and many other women from church history also fit the definition of women in church leadership.

25. Barr, *Making of Biblical Womanhood*, 63.

26. Barr, *Making of Biblical Womanhood*, 63.

27. Orjala Serrão, "Challenging Passages," 65–66.

Relevant Ramifications for Today's Church

C. S. Cowles helps clarify the context these verses were written in by explaining that "women, especially, were attracted to [a popular pagan cult] because they found in its exuberant worship complete freedom to express themselves fully in a way denied them by repressive conventional society. Consequently, they went wild."[28] He further clarifies that the women referenced in 1 Corinthians were "those who, through exuberant and chaotic speech, were creating confusion and disorder in the services."[29] We are reminded that, because of cultural mandates, "most of the women in that time were uneducated, illiterate, and totally ignorant of the Word of God. . . . They were full of questions and felt the freedom to voice them."[30] Serrão further explains these verses,

> In 1 Corinthians 14:34, the Greek says "the women," indicating a specific group of women who may be uneducated in Scripture but were used to taking the lead in the pagan mystery religion services. Paul is obviously not against women praying and preaching in worship services (see 11:5), but he is against those preaching—whether men or women—who are not instructed in the gospel.
>
> Finally, this verse uses the passive voice when talking about silence and submission, indicating a voluntary act. And it is not only for women but also for men, as found in 14:28: "Let him/her be silent in the church and let him/her speak [silently] to himself/herself and to God" (author's translation).[31]

The women in these verses, then, were invited to leave their previous pagan forms of worship behind and to appropriately engage in Christian worship while they were being instructed in the gospel. Although not an exact parallel as the context still differs, the application of these verses in today's church is more suitably extended to those, women or men, who are uneducated in the Christian faith or are causing disturbances during Christian worship services. These persons may also wisely be invited to leave their previous, non-Christian practices behind, to appropriately engage in Christian worship, and to be discipled in faith. These verses are weighty, but they do not support prohibiting women from ministry leadership positions in today's church.

---

28. Cowles, *Woman's Place?*, 131.
29. Cowles, *Woman's Place?*, 133.
30. Cowles, *Woman's Place?*, 135–36.
31. Orjala Serrão, "Challenging Passages," 66.

The context of 1 Tim 2:11–12 is similar to the text above in that it was written in a culture in which pagan religions had a negative influence. The passage reads, "Let a woman learn in silence with full submission. I permit no woman to teach or to have authority over a man; she is to keep silent." Discussing the context for this verse, Cowles explains that goddess worship and many non-Christian, gnostic gospels were especially appealing to women "in that they bestowed upon them dignity and self-esteem.... And it led women into all sorts of doctrinal and behavioral extremes."[32] He further states that "it is against this general religious background that Paul's specific instructions to women, in the verses that follow, must be read."[33] This background is important as

> the revolutionary nature of [this verse] has been utterly lost to us.... We have been conditioned to focus upon "silence" and "submissiveness." Not so the original readers. They heard Paul say something absolutely unprecedented in human history. He not only approves of women receiving instruction, being educated, but also commands it. Most translations do not give the verse the imperative force that it has in the Greek. Paul does not say that women "may learn" or "should learn" but that "a woman must learn." . . . Suggesting that women possessed the ability to learn, much less had a right to an education, shattered conventional stereotypes.[34]

Cowles clarifies that it was necessary to coach women in the proper behavior for students. This proper behavior was to quietly and respectfully listen to their instructor or to "learn in silence with full submission." Women's prior experience would not have informed them how to behave as students, as they would not previously have had such an opportunity. This silent, submissive behavior was expected for men as well as for women in educational settings.[35] Rather than correcting or restricting women, this passage presented new opportunities for them.

After reading that women are to become educated, we read a statement that seems to limit Paul's instruction in verse 12: "I permit no woman to teach or to have authority over a man." This verse sounds like a blanket statement, however, "'I am not presently permitting a woman to teach' is a

---

32. Cowles, *Woman's Place?*, 142.
33. Cowles, *Woman's Place?*, 143.
34. Cowles, *Woman's Place?*, 143.
35. Cowles, *Woman's Place?*, 144–45.

better, more accurate translation."[36] Again, because of their non-Christian background, "it is likely these mature Ephesian women were used to leading pagan temple worship . . . [but they] were teaching unorthodox lessons. It is no wonder Paul did not allow these newly converted Ephesian women to teach! He would not have allowed uneducated men to teach either."[37] Paul was not "laying down a timeless and universal principle prohibiting women from either teaching (preaching) or exercising positions of leadership in the church. . . . He was encouraging them to be submissive and quiet learners until they had been fully instructed. . . . They would then be qualified and competent to exercise the authority of one who teaches sound doctrine."[38]

In addition to women teaching in the church, in particular teaching men, the sticking point in complementarian ideology is often found in the phrase from verse 12, which says, "have authority over a man." However, even this phrase is less cut-and-dried than English translations portray. The Greek word translated as "authority" is better translated as "to domineer, lord it over."[39] "Such dominance is ruled out by Jesus in all Kingdom relationships (Mark 10:42–45). So verse 12 does not forbid women from exercising leadership . . . over men but only from domineering them in an aggressive and brazen way."[40]

Rather than universally applying this passage to all women, these verses find a more appropriate parallel in today's church to those uneducated in spiritual matters, whether they are new to the faith or not, but still speak forcefully regarding these same spiritual matters. Again, while the biblical context differs from today's, it is clear that for Paul, the adage "the loudest voice is the one that gets heard" did not hold. Instead, Paul instructed those who spoke in a domineering manner based on their non-Christian experience to take the humble position of learner. Paul graciously invited these "loud voices" into the life of the newly-established Christian church and provided a path forward for them to participate fully. Far from being a passage that either supports complementarianism or is avoided,

---

36. Orjala Serrão, "Challenging Passages," 67.
37. Orjala Serrão, "Challenging Passages," 67.
38. Cowles, *Woman's Place?*, 147.
39. Orjala Serrão, "Challenging Passages," 67.
40. Cowles, *Woman's Place?*, 146.

dismissed, or "explained away," this passage contains wisdom needed by today's church congregations and Christian culture at large.[41]

How these and other biblical passages are interpreted affects mothers in ministry leadership directly. Correct interpretations can endorse and encourage these ministers. Misinterpretations can push them away from the role God has called them to and toward the roles of submissive wife and complementarian mother instead. This is not only a loss to the individual would-be ministers and their families; it is a loss to the church as well. Those who remain in ministry regardless of these misinterpretations may be hindered in their ability to fulfill their callings, both by the complementarian and intensive mothering pressures they contend with and by the outright opposition they face. The impact of these interpretations extends well beyond those who are mothers. Church congregations' attitudes toward women in ministry leadership spills over to their attitude toward women in general and affects church culture overall.

PRACTICAL CONSIDERATIONS

These specialized ministries have the potential to be meaningful discipleship settings, however. It is essential to consider if they are discipling Christians in the image of Christ or if they are discipling Christians in intensive mothering and complementarian ideology. Even the practical elements, such as when and where these ministries are held and if childcare is available, send a message. Is it assumed that all mothers are stay-at-home moms and can meet on a weekday morning, or are there options for moms who work outside the home? Is childcare available for women's and men's events, or is it assumed that mothers will automatically cover this need during church events, but fathers will not? For those parenting classes intended for both parents, are traditional gender roles assumed, both in presentation and follow-up discussion, or are egalitarian examples shared and assumed? Who is in leadership and in which ministries? Are complementarian standards implied, or are biblical examples followed instead? Are women and men equally represented in "service" ministries such as childcare, teaching young children, funeral dinners, hospitality, and the like? Are they equally represented in visible "leadership" ministries such as preaching, teaching, and serving on leadership boards? Which people are held up as Christian examples and why? What

---

41. For an in-depth discussion on 1 Cor 14:34–35 and 1 Tim 2:11–12, see Cowles, *Woman's Place?*, 127–37.

does the above communicate about both the value of the people ministering and the value of the ministry being done, whether it be preaching or cooking? The answers to each of these questions can reveal previously unrecognized bias within local church bodies. Asking questions such as these and taking positive action in response has the potential to build a church culture in which all persons and positions of service are valued.

Another question for the church to consider is the church's attitude toward resources such as daycares, preschools, after-school care, and learning centers. While in past generations, a mother could rely on her "village" for assistance in mothering her children, these childcare versions of today's "village" have often been discouraged in American culture. This attitude has especially been true in conservative American church culture. Is today's church supportive of parents who rely on resources such as outside childcare, or is it only supportive of mothers who mother in the "one way" the church has traditionally deemed acceptable, which excludes outside childcare? When outside care is utilized, are mothers presumed to be solely responsible for arranging this childcare village, or does this responsibility extend to fathers as well? Further, what is the church's attitude toward fathers taking an equal share of the much discussed "second shift"[42] and "mental load"[43] most often carried by mothers? What of the various viewpoints on maternal gatekeeping between parents?[44] Are there examples

---

42. Douglas and Michaels explain that "in her highly influential and deeply depressing book, *The Second Shift*, Arlie Hochschild also documented that after a forty-hour (or often longer) workweek, it was Mom who scrubbed the toilets, cleaned out the moldy leftovers from the fridge, did everyone's laundry, and chauffeured kids to their soccer matches." Douglas and Michaels, *Mommy Myth*, ch. 3.

43. Lockman explains that "women and men do not develop the same 'parental consciousness' when they transition into mother- and fatherhood; they continue on separate and unequal paths of knowing or not knowing as their children change and grow. Parental consciousness is the awareness of the needs of children accompanied by the steady process of thinking about those needs. Women have come to call it the mental load." Further, "the mental load's relentless invisibility makes it hard to co-manage for two unequally motivated parties." Lockman, *All the Rage*, ch. 4.

44. Lockman explains of this viewpoint that "dads are incompetent, and moms are intolerant. It's the stuff of old commercials and lazy sitcoms. It's also got a name in academia, and that name is maternal gatekeeping. There is this gate around children, and mothers police it, keeping hapless fathers out. Or, rather, it is maternal characteristics that hinder paternal involvement." The issue is not as cut-and-dried as it first appears, as "a 2008 study out of Ohio State . . . found that when fathers held egalitarian values, mothers were more likely to facilitate their participation." Therefore, "it's hard to draw clear lines between a father's passive refusal and a mother's active constraint. Women who can't count on their partners to execute their duties in good faith may feel little

in the church of women and men modeling egalitarian parenting? Does the language used, and the examples celebrated, enable these actions? This model of parenting does not need to become the new "one way" to parent. Ideally, families will have a variety of parenting structures from which to choose. This new ideal could include stay-at-home moms or dads, parents who work outside the home either full or part-time, mothers and fathers who participate equally in family life and domestic responsibilities, and parents who incorporate a variety of combinations of these options. These steps could help Christian women successfully mother in today's culture without resorting to making mothering their primary identity.

What do those offering pastoral counseling through the church advise in this effort? In both premarital and marriage counseling sessions, are egalitarian, biblical values encouraged, over and against patriarchal, complementarian values? What relationship arrangements are shared in counseling sessions as positive examples? When couples begin having children, what gender roles are assumed or encouraged for parents? Many stereotypical gender and motherhood roles manifest once a couple has children, even for couples who previously enjoyed egalitarian gender roles. With this being the case, are couples encouraged to discuss, pre-children, their role expectations for their future with children? Further, what are churches teaching children, teens, and adults about their possible future parenting roles? What examples are shared, both positive and negative? What domestic responsibilities are being communicated as gender roles to future generations? Which roles and domestic responsibilities are children and teenagers encouraged or required to practice, and what expectations are parents encouraged by the church to set for their children? Examining questions such as these, and being intentional to act toward biblical values in response, has the potential to set expectations for church families and church culture. These expectations, once set, will significantly influence the future of mothering, both in church and society.

MODELING WITHIN THE CHURCH

What standards and mothering examples are held up in today's local church congregations? Are women who are Christian leaders in the local church modeling unrealistic standards, or are they able to authentically share their struggles with their community without fear of judgment? Are the examples

---

choice but to keep the gate." Lockman, *All the Rage*, ch. 5.

held up by leaders, such as preachers and teachers, doing the same? Are congregations made aware of historical women who did not conform to patriarchal motherhood standards but were nonetheless celebrated by the church? Could such women be addressed in small groups and Bible studies or worked into sermon illustrations? What about women like Perpetua, Monica, Paula, Dhuoda, Julian of Norwich, Jane de Chantal, Susanna Wesley, Phoebe Palmer, and Sojourner Truth, women who sacrificed in martyrdom, tearfully prayed, left behind children to follow God, educated, advised, had visions, interpreted visions, raised children in faith, preached, taught, and fought for freedom? Are there contemporary examples of women who likewise do not fully conform to intensive or complementarian motherhood standards but who can be held up as positive examples for the Christian church? Local church bodies can be intentional in who they highlight as models for women, engaging women from both the past and the present, and what actions of these women are highlighted as important. For example, do these actions prioritize the standards of intensive mothering, or are those standards allowed to be put aside in the interest of faith priorities? It is important churches communicate that it is acceptable to set aside unrealistic and unnecessary standards and provide examples of those who do so. Without this understanding, families, and mothers in particular, may try to maintain those unrealistic standards and face the cost involved, as discussed in previous chapters. Churches can further communicate examples of women who not only set aside intensive and complementarian expectations but who then prioritized following Christ over and above all other causes. These women paved the way, setting examples mothers today can follow.

Is there room in church culture for the mothers for whom motherhood standards do not apply? Where do the Hagars, Zilpahs, Bilhahs, and Sojourners connect in Christian community? For example, what about women who have been oppressed, could not keep their children, or were not expected to keep their children? What about mothers coming from complicated family structures or illicit pasts, as many of the mothers of the Bible did? Where and how do they connect with today's church as part of God's family? Are there examples of women who have overcome similar situations shared in the church? Are there examples of women still in such situations being embraced by and welcomed into the church? It is important the church welcome these women, too, as fully and equally created in the image of God, part of God's family, and part of God's church.

Much of the attitude toward motherhood and mothering within the church stems from church leadership, whether that leadership is female or male. Much of this attitude also stems from the messages received from the pulpit. Are these messages full of grace or legalism? Are there bold women willing to testify, as Phoebe Palmer did, that while they love their children, God is first in their hearts and lives? Further, are the families and churches of these bold women willing to support them in this testimony? Are there leaders willing and capable of sharing the dangers of relational idolatry, addressing it as the sin that it is, regardless of the possible cultural pushback? Will leaders be willing to highlight the problematic issues with intensive and complementarian motherhood? Are mothers, and congregations at large, being discipled to mirror Christ? Or are mothers and congregations discipled to mirror the culture around them, including the sometimes-misguided church culture? Leaders are needed within the evangelical church to push back against the cultures of intensive mothering, complementarian ideology, and relational idolatry. Leaders are needed to help disciple church congregations to place their primary identity in Christ alone.

TODAY'S REALITY

Saint Jerome's summary of motherhood still has a ring of truth, not in the lack of God but rather in the busyness of the "wife and mother" scene when he writes,

> Then come the prattling of infants, the noisy household, children watching for her word and waiting for her kiss, the reckoning up of expenses.... Meanwhile a message is delivered that the husband and his friends have arrived. The wife, like a swallow, flies all over the house. "*She has to see to everything. Is the sofa smooth? Is the pavement swept? Are the flowers in the cups? Is dinner ready?*" Tell me, pray, where amid all this is there room for the thought of God?[45]

Jerome implies the answer is no, there isn't room, and then suggests that something is indeed wrong with this scenario. Jerome, of course sees the answer as a call to celibacy and away from motherhood! But there are ancient pressures from that highly patriarchal society in late antiquity that still find their way into a mother's life today. The rise of intensive mothering and the specific patriarchal details of complementarianism can be

---

45. Jerome, *Complete Works*, sec. "Perpetual Virginity of Blessed Mary," para. 22 (italics in original).

traced throughout recent years. However, as Jerome's words suggest, the struggle with the demanding responsibilities of motherhood and the sin of relational idolatry is not new. Thankfully, as faithful women of the Bible and history demonstrate, mothers finding their identities in Christ rather than in mothering or motherhood is also not new. The way has already been paved.

The reality is that mothering will still be busy, even if the childcare village is in place, fathers are equally sharing in parenting, and today's standards are realistically reevaluated and placed in perspective. Further, while this will not be the case for every mother, many mothers will embrace the primary caretaker role, whether she decides to do this as a full-time stay-at-home mom or not. As stated above, there can be meaning and joy in this role. It is important that the church is intentional in discipling mothers and families in the various situations that make up their congregations.

THE CHURCH'S ROLE

It is essential that while the church seeks to disciple mothers away from the relational idolatry so easily connected with intensive, complementarian mothering, it does not inadvertently add another layer of expectations on mothers. That is, it is important not to merely add a standard of spiritual life on top of today's mothering standards. This only increases the burden on today's mothers when Christ calls his disciples to lay down their burdens.[46] Instead, a heart change is needed for mothers to reorient from relational idolatry, intensive mothering, and complementarian standards and toward putting Christ first in their hearts and lives. To help enable this, a perspective change is needed for all Christians away from the expectations of unrealistic motherhood ideals. For Christian mothers and other disciples, these changes can be important ways to "hear the word of God and do it." How can the church support this kind of discipleship? What other positive examples are available, and how can they be shared with mothers seeking Christ?

This discussion ends with many of the questions with which it began, hopefully offering a starting point for this conversation. How can mothers make sense of the many messages insistent on dictating how they live? How does a Christian mother determine which voices to listen to, which to dismiss, and ultimately, where her identity lies? Where does the evangelical church go from here? Again, nothing less than a full-scale, countercultural

---

46. See Matt 11:28.

change within the evangelical church can alter these intensive, complementarian motherhood ideals. What other ideas, insights, and solutions can be added to the conversation on the issues raised here? How can church attenders work together as a local church body and as the church at large to shift these deeply ingrained beliefs?

The Bible and church history are full of women who found God in the midst of mothering. They also found God in the act of mothering; they found God as Mother. Rather than being a place of oppression, striving to fit mothers into the "one way" of motherhood, the church is to be a place that sets mothers and other persons free, free to follow God's call and free from the expectations of patriarchal motherhood. Rather than mirroring secular society, it is time for the church to be as revolutionary as it was when it started and to follow in the footsteps of the early believers. It is time for the church to remove boundaries put in place by church and society, often the boundaries of patriarchal motherhood, and disciple Christians to place their identities in Christ alone. Christians today can imitate the faithful examples of mothers of the Bible and throughout history. We, the church, can build on our shared mothering legacy, allowing mothers of the past to lead the way forward. We, too, can disciple Christians to turn to God our Mother, to find and follow God in the midst of mothering, and to hear the word of God and do it.

****

Imagine the following scenario in which a couple attends church for the first time in years. What is their motivation? How would their experience unfold? What impressions would they carry with them afterward?

Chloe was at her breaking point; she was exhausted. Her full-time job kept her busy, but she had enjoyed being active for years. It wasn't until the birth of her first child four years ago that she began to feel overextended. Now, she had a full-time job, a four-year-old son, Cayden, and an eighteen-month-old daughter, Mia. Her husband Marc was sympathetic but slightly mystified by her situation. As an "involved father," he helped at home, but the responsibility to keep everything going fell on Chloe. There was always more to do, and although Marc found time to relax most evenings, Chloe couldn't seem to make this happen. She missed having downtime or any time at all for self-care, realizing this added to her daily struggle. Honestly, it also added to her feelings of guilt over not having time to address her so-called "baby weight" and continued "baby blues," well past the point she felt she should still have either.

These issues were part of why she was motivated enough to convince her husband to try out church this past Sunday. Although they had both attended as children, they had each phased out of church attendance years prior. However, Chloe recalled feeling close to God during youth group meetings and remembered how encouraging those moments had been. Those memories prompted hope that a return to church might be the help she needed. It had been nearly a decade since she had been to a worship service and even longer for Marc. Chloe began to review their recent church experience as she drove to pick up their children after work.

As they pulled into the church parking lot, the name of the pastor and the service times were listed on the digital reader board. They were a bit surprised to see a woman's name under "pastor." The screen flashed to the next frame, which read, "For a long time I have held my peace; I have kept still and restrained myself; now I will cry out like a woman in labor; I will gasp and pant. (Isaiah 42:14)." Chloe was shocked, but in a good way. She had never thought before that God could relate to her childbirth with such apparent empathy. She sighed deeply and felt strangely welcomed. Marc made some remark about how much she had screamed giving birth to their two children. Although they laughed about it later, they had quickly changed the subject when Cayden asked why she screamed.

The greeters in the church lobby were friendly and helpful, showing them the way to the nursery and how to check in on the computerized system. Chloe was invited to a moms' group that meets on a weekday morning, which she won't be able to attend because of her job. They quickly followed up, saying that there was also a group that met on Tuesday evenings for any moms who worked during the day. She appreciated the warm invitation and the church's sensitivity to working moms. One of the nursery volunteers who, judging by the toddler clinging to his leg, was also a dad about their age, struck up a short conversation with Marc. He invited Marc to an upcoming men's event, adding that childcare was available for the event. Marc's involvement in the check-in process encouraged her; it was wonderful not to feel on her own and she was glad Marc seemed happy to be at church. He even mentioned to Chloe that he would be happy to volunteer for the nursery in a church like this. Chloe privately hoped the presence of men in the nursery meant the mentality that women were automatically the primary caregivers for children was balanced a bit here. She also hoped that meant she would not be looked down upon because she and Marc used childcare during the week. With that potentially awkward social situation skirted, and feeling confident in the level of care Cayden and Mia would receive, Chloe and Marc found their way to the sanctuary.

As the musical intro played, Chloe and Marc used the QR code from the screen up front to pull up the church's website. The website was contemporary, inviting, and showed both men and women in pictures of the leaders and board members of the church. The whole experience was proving to be so much different than she anticipated that her defenses all but dropped.

The morning's worship songs included hymns familiar to both Chloe and Marc and contemporary choruses new to them. She flipped through the hymnal and noticed immediately that the editors had been careful to use inclusive language where they could. Even some of the oldest hymns were reworked. She then realized that all the language used, whether printed, spoken, or sung, followed this inclusive pattern. Chloe knew that kind of thoughtful language could not be taken for granted and felt she had been intentionally included. When both women and men came to collect the offering, Chloe and Marc looked at each other in disbelief.

The pastoral prayer was beautiful, as it acknowledged the struggles of human life and Jesus's empathy toward human frailty. God was spoken to in the prayer as a very present help, giving Chloe hope that she could make it through the stresses of her present situation. She thought immediately that this was the kind of God she wanted her own children to learn about.

Chloe remembered feeling Marc startle beside her as they prayed, caught off guard when God was referred to from the pulpit not only as "Father" but also referenced in motherly terms. She straightened her back a little as she drove and chuckled that she probably had also straightened her back during the prayer, even as her head was bowed. How refreshing to realize that the role of "mother" also represents the divine. Also, how touching, Chloe thought now, that she could have not only a "Father/Daughter" relationship with God, but also a "Mother/Daughter" one. Although she had a solid relationship with her dad, she thought of how different it was from the relationship she had with her mom, and she teared up when she put that image into the context of relating to God. While she often went to her dad for instruction or help, it was her mom she wanted whenever she was sick or sad. Most people she knew felt the same way about their moms. As far as the day-to-day went, Chloe basically told her mom everything—what a different way to relate to God! Chloe was amazed at how much that singular visit to church had already affected her, and that didn't even include the sermon!

Chloe had been hoping for encouragement through the sermon, and she was not disappointed. Apparently, it was the youth pastor's turn to preach that Sunday (which was an interesting idea—to share the pulpit). He had chosen a Scripture passage from Matt 6, which included Jesus discussing the birds of the air and the lilies of the field, calling followers to seek God first. The point was that although birds and flowers didn't work or "toil," God still fed and clothed them. Chloe wondered if the sermon had been written specifically for her that morning. It had taken the birds and lilies from the ancient Bible passage and directly connected them to today's worries about meal planning and laundry—and it wasn't even Mother's Day. Although the illustration had been expanded to include all worries in life, Chloe reflected as she drove that these tasks were part of what was overwhelming her, causing her to seek help in the first place. It seemed she truly had gone to the right place. God was portrayed as one who truly loved them and wanted to be an integral part of their lives. Was it possible that God would care for her, too, just as God cared for the birds and the lilies? Could she also be called to seek God first? Something stirred within her; Marc seemed to be having a similar experience.

Between the nursery check-in, the messaging in the service, the prayer, and the pastor's comments, Chloe began feeling that this could be a place that would truly and genuinely help them. She would not have to wonder if others were thinking she needed to spend more time becoming a better wife and mother. She sensed a freedom to be herself, that she could come to this place and be honest about her need for a full night's sleep! Chloe supported her family and had come to church that morning hoping for some support for herself. Marc also seemed to be reaching the place of acknowledging that they needed help, even if it was as simple as seeing these people as a model, as ones who had walked the path of parenthood already. He reflected that besides his parents, he really didn't even know people who were a generation older. What could he learn from them? After the service, people continued to engage with them. Marc excused himself from conversation to go get the kids from the nursery.

As Chloe neared the end of the commute to their childcare center, she reflected on how easy it was to get pulled into that loving community. Although she couldn't name it, Chloe had begun to reawaken to faith and had been hopeful for a renewed relationship with God through church involvement. After her recent experience, she reflected that although she was still exhausted as a working mom, that renewed relationship with God had already begun. She felt a weight had been lifted and concluded that the spiritual experiences she remembered from her teenage years had been right on track; the church was a source of encouragement and help. It was a good start; there was no doubt that they would return to that church the following Sunday. Even as she mentally prepared to pick up her high-energy children and for the start of her "second shift," she smiled in anticipation.

Bibliography

1in6. "The 1 in 6 Statistic." https://1in6.org/statistic/.
The Ante-Nicene Fathers. Edited by Alexander Roberts and James Donaldson. 1885–1887. 10 vols. Repr., Peabody, MA: Hendrickson, 1994.
Augustine. *The Works of Saint Augustine: A Translation for the 21st Century*. Edited by John E. Rotelle. Translated by Maria Boulding. Hyde Park, NY: New City, 1997. Kindle.
Barr, Beth Allison. *The Making of Biblical Womanhood: How the Subjugation of Women Became Gospel Truth*. Grand Rapids: Brazos, 2021.
Belkin, Lisa. "The Opt-Out Revolution." *New York Times*, Oct. 26, 2003. https://www.nytimes.com/2003/10/26/magazine/the-opt-out-revolution.html.
Billman, Kathleen D., and Daniel L. Migliore. *Rachel's Cry: Prayer of Lament and Rebirth of Hope*. Eugene, OR: Wipf & Stock, 2007.
Bowler, Kate. *The Preacher's Wife: The Precarious Power of Evangelical Women Celebrities*. Princeton: Princeton University Press, 2019. Kindle.
Boyd, Kayla, and Nicole Pomarico. "30 Mommy Influencers Every Fellow Mom Should Follow." Cafe Mom, Mar. 1, 2021. https://cafemom.com/parenting/mommy-influencers-we-love.
Brenner, Athalya, and Fokkelien Van Dijk-Hemmes. *On Gendering Texts: Female and Male Voices in the Hebrew Bible*. Biblical Interpretation Series 1. Leiden: Brill, 1993.
Bronner, Leila Leah. *Stories of Biblical Mothers: Maternal Power in the Hebrew Bible*. Dallas, TX: University Press of America, 2004.
Brown, Raymond. *The Birth of the Messiah*. Garden City, NY: Doubleday, 1977.
Buckhanon Crowder, Stephanie. *When Momma Speaks: The Bible and Motherhood from a Womanist Perspective*. Louisville: Westminster John Knox, 2016. Kindle.
Bulkeley, Tim. *Not Only a Father: Talk of God as Mother in the Bible and Christian Tradition*. Auckland, New Zealand: Archer, 2011.
Bynum, Caroline Walker. *Jesus as Mother: Studies in the Spirituality of the High Middle Ages*. Berkeley: University of California Press, 1982.
Byrd, Aimee. *Recovering from Biblical Manhood and Womanhood: How the Church Needs to Rediscover Her Purpose*. Grand Rapids: Zondervan Reflective, 2020. Kindle.
Chilcote, Paul W. *She Offered Them Christ: The Legacy of Women Preachers in Early Methodism*. Nashville: Abingdon, 1993.

Bibliography

Church of the Nazarene. *Manual 2017–2021: History, Constitution, Government, Sacraments, and Rituals.* Kansas City, MO: Nazarene, 2017. Kindle.

———. "Nazarene Missions International History." https://nazarene.org/who-we-are/organization/ministries/nazarene-missions-international/who-we-are/nmi-history.

Claassens, L. Juliana M. *The God Who Provides: Biblical Images of Divine Nourishment.* Nashville: Abingdon, 2004.

———. *Mourner, Mother, Midwife: Reimagining God's Delivering Presence in the Old Testament.* Louisville: Westminster John Knox, 2012.

Clanton, Jann Aldredge. *In Whose Image?* New York: Crossroad, 1990.

Clark, Gillian. *Monica: An Ordinary Saint.* New York: Oxford University Press, 2015.

Coleson, Joseph E. *Ezer Cenegdo: A Power Like Him, Facing Him as Equal.* Grantham, PA: Wesleyan/Holiness Women Clergy, 1996.

Cook, Joan E. *Hannah's Desire, God's Design: Early Interpretations of the Story of Hannah.* Sheffield: Sheffield Academic, 1999.

Cowles, C. S. *A Woman's Place? Leadership in the Church.* Kansas City: Beacon Hill, 1993.

Cristiani, Leon. *The Story of Monica and Her Son Augustine (331–387).* Translated by Angeline Bouchard. Boston, MA: Daughters of St. Paul, 1977.

Derck, Sarah Coleson. "Wisdom from the Old Testament." In *Faithful to the Call: Women in Ministry*, edited by Carla D. Sunberg, 71–84. Kansas City, MO: Foundry, 2022.

Dille, Sarah J. *Mixing Metaphors: God as Mother and Father in Deutero-Isaiah.* New York: T&T Clark, 2004.

Douglas, Susan J., and Meredith W. Michaels. *The Mommy Myth: The Idealization of Motherhood and How It Has Undermined Women.* New York: Free Press, 2004. Kindle.

Eastman, Susan. *Recovering Paul's Mother Tongue: Language and Theology in Galatians.* Grand Rapids: Eerdmans, 2007.

Farley, Wendy. *The Thirst of God: Contemplating God's Love with Three Women Mystics.* Louisville: Westminster John Knox, 2015. http://ebookcentral.proquest.com/lib/nts-ebooks/detail.action?docID=3446612.

Frymer-Kensky, Tikva. *Reading the Women of the Bible: A New Interpretation of Their Stories.* New York: Schocken, 2002.

Gafney, Wilda C. *Womanist Midrash: A Reintroduction to the Women of the Torah and the Throne.* Louisville: Westminster John Knox, 2017.

Gaventa, Beverly Roberts. *Mary: Glimpses of the Mother of Jesus.* Minneapolis: Fortress, 1995.

———. *Our Mother Saint Paul.* Louisville: Westminster John Knox, 2007. Kindle.

Gaventa, Beverly Roberts, and Cynthia L. Rigby, eds. *Blessed One: Protestant Perspectives on Mary.* Louisville: Westminster John Knox, 2002.

Gies, Frances, and Joseph Gies. *Marriage and the Family in the Middle Ages.* New York: Harper & Row, 1987.

Gupta, Alisha Haridasani. "Covid Shuttered Schools Everywhere. So Why Was the 'She-Cession' Worse in the U.S.?" *New York Times*, May 28, 2021. https://www.nytimes.com/2021/05/28/us/shecession-america-europe-child-care.html.

Gutiérrez, Gustavo. *We Drink from Our Own Wells: The Spiritual Journey of a People.* Translated by Matthew J. O'Connell. Maryknoll, NY: Orbis, 2003.

Hays, Sharon. *The Cultural Contradictions of Motherhood.* New Haven: Yale University Press, 1996.

Bibliography

Hess, Amanda. "Mommy Is Going Away for a While." *New York Times*, Jan. 20, 2022. https://www.nytimes.com/2022/01/14/movies/bad-moms-lost-daughter.html.

Hovet, Theodore. "Phoebe Palmer's 'Altar Phraseology' and the Spiritual Dimension of Woman's Sphere." *The Journal of Religion* 63 (1983) 264–80.

Ingersol, Stan, et al. *Our Watchword and Song: The Centennial History of the Church of the Nazarene*. Edited by Floyd T. Cunningham. Kansas City: Beacon Hill, 2009.

Japinga, Lynn. *Feminism and Christianity: An Essential Guide*. Nashville: Abingdon, 1999.

———. *Preaching the Women of the Old Testament: Who They Were and Why They Matter*. Louisville: Westminster John Knox, 2017.

Jerome. *The Complete Works of Saint Jerome*. Translated by Philip Schaff. Toronto, Canada: Amazon, 2016. Kindle.

Jezer-Morton, Kathryn. "Did Moms Exist Before Social Media." *New York Times*, Apr. 16, 2020. https://www.nytimes.com/2020/04/16/parenting/mommy-influencers.html.

Johnson, Elizabeth A. *She Who Is: The Mystery of God in Feminist Theological Discourse*. New York: Crossroad, 1993.

Julian of Norwich. *Julian of Norwich: Showings*. Translated by Edmund Colledge and James Walsh. New York: Paulist, 1978.

Kempe, Margery. *The Book of Margery Kempe: The Autobiography of the Madwoman of God*. Translated by Tony D. Triggs. Liguori, MO: Triumph, 1995.

Lapsley, Jacqueline E. *Whispering the Word: Hearing Women's Stories in the Old Testament*. Louisville: Westminster John Knox, 2005.

Leclerc, Diane. *Discovering Christian Holiness: The Heart of Wesleyan-Holiness Theology*. Kansas City: Beacon Hill, 2010.

———. "'Purified Through Fire': The Piety and Power of Female Afflictions." In *Awakening to Justice: Faithful Voices from the Abolitionist Past*, edited by Doug Strong et al., 110–27. Downers Grove, IL: InterVarsity, 2024.

———. *Singleness of Heart: Gender, Sin, and Holiness in Historical Perspective*. Lanham, MD: Scarecrow, 2001.

Leclerc, Diane, and Brent Peterson. *The Back Side of the Cross: An Atonement Theology for the Abused and Abandoned*. Eugene, OR: Cascade, 2022.

Leyser, Conrad, and Lesley Smith, eds. *Motherhood, Religion, and Society in Medieval Europe, 400–1400: Essays Presented to Henrietta Leyser*. Burlington, VT: Ashgate, 2011.

Lockman, Darcy. *All the Rage: Mothers, Fathers, and the Myth of Equal Partnership*. New York: Harper Perennial, 2020. Kindle.

MacHaffie, Barbara. *Her Story: Women in Christian Tradition*. Philadelphia: Fortress, 1986.

Malherbe, Abraham J. *The Letters to the Thessalonians: A New Translation with Introduction and Commentary*. New York: Doubleday, 2000.

Marga, Amy E. *In the Image of Her: Recovering Motherhood in the Christian Tradition*. Waco, TX: Baylor University Press, 2022.

Massyngberde Ford, J. *Redeemer—Friend and Mother: Salvation in Antiquity and in the Gospel of John*. Minneapolis: Fortress, 1997.

McKnight, Scot. *The Jesus Creed: Loving God, Loving Others*. Brewster, MA: Paraclete, 2004.

McNeel, Jennifer Houston. *Paul as Infant and Nursing Mother: Metaphor, Rhetoric, and Identity in 1 Thessalonians 2:5–8*. Atlanta: SBL, 2014.

Metaxas, Eric. *7 Women: And the Secret of Their Greatness*. Nashville: Nelson, 2015.

Bibliography

Meyers, Carol. *Rediscovering Eve: Ancient Israelite Women in Context*. New York: Oxford University Press, 2013.

Miller-McLemore, Bonnie J. *Also a Mother: Work and Family as Theological Dilemma*. Nashville: Abingdon, 1994.

Myers, Alicia D. *Blessed Among Women? Mothers and Motherhood in the New Testament*. New York: Oxford University Press, 2017.

National Women's Law Center. "The Jobs Report Shows a Strong Month, But Black Women's Labor Force Participation Drops and Unemployment Rate Rises." Mar. 4, 2022. https://nwlc.org/resource/the-jobs-report-shows-a-strong-month-but-black-womens-labor-force-participation-drops-and-unemployment-rate-rises/.

Newsom, Carol A., et al., eds. *Women's Bible Commentary*. 3rd ed. Louisville: Westminster John Knox, 2012.

Ng, Sik Hung. "Androcentric Coding of *Man* and *His* in Memory by Language Users." *Journal of Experimental Social Psychology* 26 (1990) 455–64.

Niebuhr, Reinhold. *Human Nature*. Vol. 1 of *The Nature and Destiny of Man: A Christian Interpretation*. Louisville: Westminster John Knox, 1996.

Orjala Serrão, C. Jeanne. "Tackling the Challenging Passages in the New Testament." In *Faithful to the Call: Women in Ministry*, edited by Carla D. Sunberg, 55–70. Kansas City, MO: Foundry, 2022.

Palliser, Margaret A. *Christ, Our Mother of Mercy: Divine Mercy and Compassion in the Theology of the "Shewings" of Julian of Norwich*. Boston: De Gruyter, 2017.

Piper, John, and Wayne Grudem, eds. *Recovering Biblical Manhood and Womanhood: A Response to Evangelical Feminism*. Wheaton, IL: Crossway, 1991.

Rich, Adrienne. *Of Woman Born: Motherhood As Experience and Institution*. New York: Norton, 1976.

Richards, Amy. *Opting In: Having a Child Without Losing Yourself*. New York: Farrar, Straus, and Giroux, 2008. Kindle.

Schulte, Brigid. *Overwhelmed: Work, Love, and Play When No One Has the Time*. New York: Sarah Crichton, 2014.

Smith, Paul R. *Is It Okay to Call God "Mother"? Considering the Feminine Face of God*. Peabody, MA: Hendrickson, 1993.

Sri, Edward. *Rethinking Mary in the New Testament*. Greenwood Village, CO: Augustine Institute, 2006.

Stovell, Beth M., ed. *Making Sense of Motherhood: Biblical and Theological Perspectives*. Eugene, OR: Wipf & Stock, 2016.

Sunberg, Carla D., ed. *Faithful to the Call: Women in Ministry*. Kansas City, MO: Foundry, 2022.

Tertullianus, Quintus. *Tertullian: Ad Martyras and The Passion of The Holy Martyrs Perpetua and Felicitas*. Savage, MN: Lighthouse, 2016.

Tillich, Paul. *Existence and the Christ*. Vol. 2 of *Systematic Theology*. Chicago: University of Chicago Press, 1975.

Tracy, Larissa. *Women of the "Gilte Legende": A Selection of Middle English Saints Lives*. Rochester, NY: D. S. Brewer, 2012. Kindle.

Truth, Sojourner. *Ain't I a Woman?* New York: Penguin, 2020.

———. *The Narrative of Sojourner Truth: A Northern Slave, Emancipated from Bodily Servitude by the State of New York, in 1828*. Edited by Olive Gilbert. Boston: Sojourner Truth, 1850. https://digital.library.upenn.edu/women/truth/1850/1850.html.

Bibliography

Tyson, John R., ed. *Invitation to Christian Spirituality: An Ecumenical Anthology*. New York: Oxford University Press, 1999.

UN Women. "1 in 3 Women." https://data.unwomen.org/global-database-on-violence-against-women#:~:text=1%20in%203%20women,current%20or%20former%20intimate%20partners.

USAFACTS. "What Is the Labor Force Participation Rate in the US." May 2, 2025. https://usafacts.org/articles/women-now-majority-workers-payroll-bls-december-2019/.

Van Wijk-Bos, Johanna W. H. *Reimagining God: The Case for Scriptural Diversity*. Louisville: Westminster John Knox, 1995.

Vandenberg-Daves, Jodi. *Modern Motherhood: An American History*. Piscataway, NJ: Rutgers University Press, 2014.

Warner, Judith. "The Opt-Out Generation Wants Back In." *New York Times*, Aug. 7, 2013. https://www.nytimes.com/2013/08/11/magazine/the-opt-out-generation-wants-back-in.html.

Wheatley, Richard. *The Life and Letters of Mrs. Phoebe Palmer*. Miami, FL: HardPress, 2017. Kindle.

Willimon, William. *The Service of God: How Worship and Ethics Are Related*. Nashville: Abingdon, 1983.

Witherington, Ben, III. "The Waters of Birth: John 3:5 and 1 John 5:6–8." *New Testament Studies* 35 (1989) 155–60.

Wright, Wendy M. *Francis de Sales and Jane de Chantal*. Boston, MA: Pauline, 2017.

———. "Salesian Spirituality." Lecture, Nazarene Theological Seminary, Oct. 8, 2021, Kansas City, MO, Zoom.

Wylie, Philip. *Generation of Vipers*. New York: Rinehart, 1942.

www.ingramcontent.com/pod-product-compliance
Lightning Source LLC
Chambersburg PA
CBHW072137160426
43197CB00012B/2146